Measuring Pupil Achievement and Aptitude

THE PROFESSIONAL EDUCATION FOR TEACHERS SERIES

Under the Editorship of PAUL WOODRING

Editor of the Educational Supplement of the Saturday Review
and Distinguished Service Professor at Western Washington State College

PUBLISHED TITLES

Introduction to American Education, Paul Woodring

Education and Democratic Ideals, Gordon C. Lee

Education in Western Culture, Robert Ulich

American Secondary Schools, Mauritz Johnson, Jr.

Teaching in a World of Change, Robert H. Anderson

Measuring Pupil Achievement and Aptitude, C. M. Lindvall

Volumes on the following topics are in preparation: Elementary Education, Human Growth and Development, Learning in the Schools, Social Psychology in Education.

Measuring Pupil

Achievement and Aptitude

C. M. LINDVALL
University of Pittsburgh

Harcourt, Brace & World, Inc.
New York, Chicago, San Francisco, Atlanta

ISBN: 0-15-557791-3

Library of Congress Catalog Card Number: 66-25138

Printed in the United States of America

Editor's Foreword

The twentieth century has seen the development of a vast array of sophisticated instruments for the measurement of human aptitude, interest, achievement, and traits of personality. Although good teachers of earlier centuries were aware of individual differences and attempted to judge them by oral quizzes, essay examinations, and casual observations of performance, it has been only in the past fifty or sixty years that educators and psychologists have given close attention to the problems of defining objectives, identifying criteria, and establishing the reliability and validity of the measuring instruments.

If these instruments are to be fully utilized in the improvement of education, it is essential that all teachers be aware of both their potentialities and their limitations. The beginning teacher cannot be expected to be familiar with all the advanced statistical procedures used in test construction and analysis. But he should be aware of the wide variety of testing instruments available to him. He should be able to select wisely from among them, to use them properly, and to interpret the results accurately. And, because of the potential dangers in the misuse of tests, he must know which of the testing instruments cannot properly be used by a teacher who has not had advanced training in clinical psychology.

In addition to the standardized tests made by others every teacher finds it necessary to make tests of his own for classroom use. The construction of such instruments and the evaluation of student responses to them require a substantial knowledge of psychological principles and at least an elementary understanding of statistics. In addition to the tests that can be scored objectively a good teacher makes use of many evaluative procedures that must be interpreted subjectively. He should be aware of both the possibilities and the dangers of such interpretation.

Dr. Lindvall is the author of advanced and comprehensive works on testing and evaluation. In preparing this volume he has selected from a vast literature the most appropriate and useful data for the beginning teacher. He has supplemented the data on evaluation with a brief but clear and understandable introduction to statistical procedures. He has kept the needs of the teacher clearly in mind while drawing upon his own experience as a high school teacher, professor of education, and Associate Director of the Learning Research Center at the University of Pittsburgh.

Instructors may use this book in a variety of ways. If the sequence of required courses for teachers includes a unit on testing in a comprehensive introduction to education course, this volume may be used in conjunction with several others in the present series. Where the subject of testing is a part of a course in educational psychology, this book may be combined with the volumes on learning, on human growth and development, and on social psychology. Where the college offers a separate short course on testing and evaluation, this book may be used as the basic text and supplemented with as much outside reading as time permits. The paperback series of inexpensive but authoritative volumes makes possible an endless series of combinations, depending on the course organization preferred by the faculty of each individual institution.

Regardless of how the course sequence is organized, the student who makes use of this book will have moved a long way toward gaining the understanding of testing and evaluation that he will need when he enters the classroom as a teacher. If he later moves on to more advanced courses in preparation for work as a specialist, he will have a firm and scholarly base on which to build.

PAUL WOODRING

Preface

This book provides an introduction to those basic principles of testing and evaluation that every teacher should know in order to assess pupil achievement and aptitude effectively. It discusses the role of tests in education, the need for specific objectives, and the considerations that should determine the choice of tests; it describes the various kinds of tests with instructions for their preparation and use. It includes the statistical knowledge essential for understanding scoring; it has a chapter on standardized tests and one on aptitude tests. The final chapter gives practical ways of using an evaluation program.

Any textbook or course designed to give teachers a basic mastery of testing techniques within the limited time typically assigned to this topic must compromise between the desirable and the possible. Since the turn of the century, psychologists, psychometricians, and educators have developed an extensive body of measurement theory, procedures for the development of tests, and statistical techniques for the detailed analysis of tests and test results. This theory constitutes what may be the most technical body of content relevant to teaching. To master any large proportion of it would require several courses in the content itself plus a number of prerequisite courses in mathematics and statistics. Although it would be desirable for every professionally trained teacher to master this content, the limited time devoted to professional course work in teacher preparation means that most teachers can be given only an introduction to basic topics in testing.

The beginner should recognize, therefore, that what is presented in this text is but an introduction to a broad and rather technical subject. Professional educators will wish to study the topics more intensively. Some may find it possible to do advanced course work in psychological testing, measurement theory, and statistics. Those wishing to undertake a more intensive study while using this text may make use of the specific references cited at the end of each chapter. These have been selected to provide students with sources that range from the relatively simple to the rather complex. By using those sources that seem appropriate the student or the instructor can enrich the material of this text.

At certain points in this book the reader will note rather strong suggestions that the typical teacher *not* use certain instruments or procedures. These suggestions may be of far greater importance than many suggestions for what should be used. Greater harm may result when teachers attempt to employ instruments that they are not prepared to use than would result from failure to apply certain useful procedures. Many available tests can be administered and evaluated correctly only by the highly trained psychologist. For the typical teacher to concern himself with such tests can only result in misuse.

The reader who is familiar with my earlier text, *Testing and Evaluation: An Introduction* (Harcourt, Brace & World, 1961), will recognize that many of the points emphasized in that volume are also given major attention here. This emphasis continues the stress on those principles and practices that will contribute most to an improvement in the classroom use of tests and other evaluation procedures. At the same time the present text includes many significant ideas that have developed in recent years. I hope that this combination of older, established principles and promising, recent developments will provide the reader with a useful and meaningful introduction to an important area of study.

C. M. LINDVALL

Contents

Measuring Pupil Achievement and Aptitude

Chapter One

The Role of Tests
in Education

To the newcomer to teaching, testing may seem to need no introduction. During many years as a student, he has been intimately acquainted with examinations of many types. However, the teacher's understanding of tests must be quite different from that of the student. This book introduces the teacher and prospective teacher to a variety of procedures that can be used to obtain information about his students. Since testing is the major means of obtaining such information, this text will concentrate on the many types of tests used in our schools. If the teacher is to make the most effective use of tests and related data-gathering procedures, he must have a clear picture of their role in education as well as a command of the theory and technique needed to create, choose, and evaluate them.

The essential purpose of teaching is to produce changes in pupils. Any program of instruction must be based upon and be guided by information concerning pupil aptitude, interest, and achievement. A father who is teaching his son how to swim plans his teaching steps on the basis of what he knows about the child. These steps will follow one pattern if the son seems to love to be in the water, has no fear of it, and has a close friend who is already able to swim. The steps will probably be quite different if the son really fears the water and has no desire whatsoever to learn how to swim. His son's present abilities and aptitudes will also influence the father's decision as to how he will proceed. A child who has shown a capacity for learning physical tasks quickly and easily may not be taken through all the steps that would be required of a child with less aptitude. Also, as the instruction progresses, the achievement that the child has displayed in mastering previous steps will determine what will be done next. Throughout, the father's instruction will be guided by his perceptions of his son's attitude, aptitude, and achievement.

In a similar fashion, the classroom teacher should be guided by continuous information about pupil aptitude, interest, and progress. If a teacher has only one student on whom he concentrates all his attention, he may be able to obtain all the information he needs through an intensive informal observation. However, since the typical teacher must collect such information on a large number of students, he does not have the opportunity for an intensive personal observation of each. He frequently needs to use a more efficient and economical method for securing the necessary knowledge.

To return to our swimming analogy, if a swimming instructor teaches a whole class of nonswimmers rather than a single individual, he cannot possibly learn everything he needs to know about each one merely by observing the general behavior of each as the class splashes around in the pool. He probably will find it necessary to have some regular procedure for observing students while they are performing certain standard tasks. For example, to learn something about pupil readiness and aptitude, he might ask each student to jump into the water from the edge of the pool, to walk out into the deeper water until it reaches his waistline, and to lift his feet from the bottom of the pool so that he floats in a face-down, prone position. By asking each student to perform simple standard tasks of this type, the instructor can obtain a record of what each student can and will do. He could obtain the same type of information through casual observation if he were dealing with only one student, but large-group instruction demands more formal procedures if information on all students is to be obtained within the available period of time.

In the same way, every classroom teacher, although he employs as much informal observation as possible as a means of acquiring information about his pupils, also finds it necessary to use more formal procedures such as testing and other evaluation techniques. Some of these procedures may be quite similar to those used by our hypothetical swimming instructor. Pupils may be asked to carry out certain set tasks while the teacher observes the quality of each performance. In this case the teacher is using performance-type tests. Other procedures may involve paper-and-pencil tasks such as are found on a typical essay or objective-type examination. All these procedures receive major emphasis in the study of theory and technique in testing and evaluation. However, it is essential to remember that the procedures are of no value in and of themselves; they are merely refined techniques that are used to obtain necessary information about pupils. Tests are of value only if they yield information that is used to improve the total teaching-learning process.

AREAS OF PUPIL EVALUATION

The major pupil variables in educational testing and evaluation are typically grouped into four broad categories: (1) achievement, (2) aptitude, (3) interest, and (4) personality. The following sections provide an overview of the problems and procedures in each of these categories and indicate the extent to which each will be explored in this text.

Assessing Pupil Achievement. Quite obviously the classroom teacher must continually assess the level of pupil achievement. The teacher's major "business" is to produce changes in pupils, and he can determine his degree of success only by making regular assessments of what his pupils have learned. In evaluating achievement a variety of procedures will be used:

1. Nontesting procedures All teachers make some use of relatively informal procedures for determining what pupils have learned. They watch pupils perform in class; they listen to them recite; and they grade homework assignments. Although most teachers choose to supplement such techniques with more reliable and objective procedures, the obvious validity of many nontesting procedures makes them important tools for the teacher. Therefore this text will devote some attention to suggestions for the improved use of these techniques.

2. Teacher-made tests A traditional and essential tool of the classroom teacher is the teacher-made test, undoubtedly the most widely used procedure for assessing pupil achievement. Although many teachers produce excellent tests, most would agree on the basis of their experience as students that there is much room for improvement. Because of the important role of teacher-made tests, this textbook devotes considerable attention to the construction of such examinations and the use of their results.

3. Published achievement tests Although classroom achievement is most frequently evaluated through the use of teacher-devised procedures, good standardized achievement tests can be valuable for certain purposes. However, a teacher should be able to judge the worth of any such tests and know something about how the results should and should not be used. In order to choose the best published tests, a teacher should be familiar with the recommended steps to be followed in constructing a standardized test and should understand the statistical procedures used in deriving scores and in assessing the reliability and validity of the instrument. Since the classroom teacher must be prepared both to make proper use of such devices and to avoid many common misuses, these tests are an important topic in this text.

Determining Pupil Aptitude. Teacher planning of any instructional activity must take into account pupil aptitude for that type of learning. A teacher obtains much information on pupil aptitude through procedures other than tests. Certainly one of the best indicators of aptitude for study in a given subject is past performance in that subject. A teacher planning arithmetic instruction for sixth-grade students will want to know how these students did in arithmetic in fifth grade. A chemistry teacher at the end of the first month of instruction learns quite a bit about his students' aptitudes by noting their achievement up to that point. Also, teachers discover much about pupil aptitude by observing and listening to students as they work and perform in class.

But nontesting procedures, although they must be used by all teachers, are not always sufficient, nor are they in many cases the most efficient or the most valid sources of information. For some students, true aptitude for a given subject may not manifest itself in classroom performance; a student may have a latent aptitude that is not being aroused by a certain type of instruction. Also, letting an unselected group of students proceed through much of a course before testing their aptitudes will be an inefficient use of both pupil and teacher time. For such reasons as these, good aptitude tests can result in more effective instruction.

1. General scholastic aptitude or intelligence tests All students take a number of intelligence tests at selected stages in their school careers. If the results from these tests are used with care and with an understanding of what they do and do not measure, they can be a real help to guidance counselors, to school administrators, and to the classroom teacher. On the other hand, if the results of intelligence tests are improperly interpreted, it is quite easy to make incorrect and even harmful decisions on the basis of scores from intelligence tests. Certain basic understandings are necessary if teachers are to use these tests to serve the important and useful purposes for which they are intended and avoid the all-too-common misuses.

2. *Readiness tests*   One special type of aptitude test, used principally in kindergarten and first grade, is the readiness test. This test is designed specifically to determine a pupil's readiness or aptitude for beginning formal school instruction. Since the principal subject to which a student is exposed in his first year or two of schooling is reading, many of these tests measure aptitude for this one subject only and are appropriately called reading-readiness tests. Other instruments measure readiness in several areas, such as reading, arithmetic, and writing. In general, kindergarten and first-grade teachers have found readiness tests to be a useful supplement to both intelligence tests and informal procedures in making decisions as to when a pupil is ready to profit from formal instruction.

3. *Tests of aptitude for specific subjects or vocations*   At certain times in a pupil's school career, he must decide what courses he should take or what type of vocation would be a reasonable goal for him. Of course, such decisions are made on the basis of a variety of types of information, and it is doubtful that any one test score should be a major determining factor. However, tests have been developed that measure aptitude for a given subject or for a given line of work, and the results of such tests may be of some value in decision-making. But, since the validity of aptitude tests varies greatly from test to test and from one criterion to another and since data on validity are generally presented in a somewhat technical form, all educators should know how to evaluate specific aptitude tests.

Determining Pupil Interests.   Of considerable importance in educational and vocational planning is knowledge of a pupil's interests. Again, much information will be obtained by the teacher, the parent, and the pupil himself through informal assessments. However, there are a number of tests or inventories that provide relatively objective procedures for determining interest. Such instruments, typically described as measuring *interest* or *preference,* can be used as aids to further explorations of pupil interests through personal counseling sessions. The publishers of these devices usually caution the user not to take the results as an absolute measure of interest that can be used for making arbitrary decisions about areas in which pupils could be expected to find satisfaction and success. The beginning teacher should be warned to use the test results only under the direction of a guidance counselor or other person with considerable training and experience in their interpretation. Since interest inventories are not an essential tool of the typical classroom teacher and should be used only with the qualifications described above, they are not discussed in any detail in this text.

Assessing Pupil Personality. There are many published instruments for assessing personality. These are variously described as inventories, schedules, records, profiles, check lists, surveys, and tests, and their titles suggest that they measure such things as temperament, personality, problems, preferences, values, and attitudes. Many of these devices can be quite helpful when used judiciously by a trained psychologist or counselor. However, the rather indiscriminate use of these instruments by a teacher without special training may actually aggravate the problems they were intended to help solve. In view of the present techniques for assessing personality, it is the writer's judgment that these instruments should not be used by the classroom teacher but rather left to the clinical psychologist and the researcher. For this reason they are not dealt with in this text.

CRITICISMS OF TESTING

This chapter has emphasized that educational and psychological tests can be valuable tools for improving education. However, as with any tool, tests must be selected with care and used with skill and understanding. The past half-century has seen the development of many worthwhile tests that have been wisely used by a number of educators. At the same time, many ineffective tests have also been produced, and poorly informed educators have improperly used even the good tests.

In recent years a variety of criticisms of tests and testing have appeared as books and as articles in popular journals. Some critics have disapproved of testing in general; some have been concerned about using tests in business and industry; some have condemned the practice of relying exclusively on tests in awarding scholarships; others have denounced the use of objective-type test items. Many of these critics make important and valid points. There is no doubt that many tests contain some poor items, and certain present-day test uses should be questioned. The truly professional teacher is aware of test limitations and is alert to the possibility of test misuse. When developing or selecting a test for a given purpose, he recognizes its limitations and asks himself if alternative procedures would be more effective. For example, a given achievement test, although appearing to be quite valid for his purpose, may have a few items of questionable value. In this situation he will ask himself if alternative methods for obtaining information about pupil achievement would be more valid and reliable. The decision is not the simple one of deciding whether to use a given test, but rather of deciding what procedure for gaining information about pupils will be most valuable in improving instruction.

The basic problem in the selection and proper use of tests was discussed quite clearly in an editorial appearing in *Science,* a publication of the American Association for the Advancement of Science; it stated in part:

> All informed predictions of future performance are based upon some knowledge of relevant past performance; school grades, research productivity, sales records, batting averages, or whatever is appropriate. How well the predictions will be validated by later performance depends upon the amount, reliability, and appropriateness of the information used and on the skill and wisdom with which it is interpreted. Anyone who keeps careful score knows that the information available is always incomplete and that the predictions are always subject to error.
>
> Whether to use tests, other kinds of information, or both in a particular situation depends, therefore, upon the empirical evidence concerning comparative validity, and upon such factors as cost and availability.
>
> Professionals in the business and the conscientious publishers know the limitations as well as the values. They write these things into test manuals and in critiques of available tests. But they have no jurisdiction over users; an educational test can be administered by almost anyone, whether he knows how to interpret it or not.
>
> In the long run it may be possible to establish better controls or

to require higher qualifications. But in the meantime, unhappily, the demonstrated value of these tests under many circumstances has given them a popularity that has led to considerable misuse. Also, unhappily, justifiable criticism of the misuse now threatens to hamper proper use. Business and government can probably look after themselves. But school guidance and selection programs are being attacked for using a valuable tool, because some of the users are unskilled.[1]

SUMMARY

Tests and other procedures for assessing pupil achievement and aptitude are essential tools of the educator. However, tests are valuable only if they are properly constructed and if the results are correctly evaluated and used to improve teaching methods. The theory and techniques that have been developed in testing and measurement constitute some of the more complex and technical content encountered by the professional educator. This book merely introduces the reader to certain key topics in effective testing; it covers the skills and understandings that are essential in preparing the beginning classroom teacher. Every teacher should be able to make effective use of a variety of procedures and devices for determining aptitude and achievement. But every teacher should also learn how to avoid misusing tests and should recognize that many readily obtainable instruments such as those for measuring personality and interest are better left for use by the psychologist and guidance counselor.

Suggestions for Class Discussion and Further Investigation

1. Assume that you are a teacher in a classroom situation in which you are not able to use any written tests, either essay or objective-type, but must rely solely on class discussion and on the observation of pupil performance to evaluate pupil achievement. What would be some of the difficulties you would face?
2. Assume that you are a pupil in the classroom described in suggestion 1 and that the teacher is going to determine your course grade solely on the basis of how you answer questions during class discussion. List some of the objections you would have to using this procedure.

---

1. From "Educational Tests," *Science* (December 20, 1963).

3. As a pupil you have taken many teacher-made achievement tests. List some of your most common complaints about these tests and the ways in which they were used. As you proceed through this text develop a list of suggestions that you might follow to avoid identical student complaints about your own tests.

4. Imagine that you are assigned to teach a subject in which you are competent to a student who is a complete stranger to you. What types of information about this student would be valuable to you before you started teaching? What information could be secured through a test? What information could not be secured from a test?

Suggestions for Further Reading

To understand present practices in testing and evaluation it is important to know something about the historical development of this field. The following sources give brief but informative descriptions of this history: Anne Anastasi, *Psychological Testing,* 2nd ed. (New York: Macmillan, 1961); Leonard P. Ayres, "History and Present Status of Educational Measurements," *The Measurement of Educational Products,* 17th Yearbook of the National Society for the Study of Education (Bloomington, Ill.: Public School Publishing Co., 1922); Henry Chauncey and John E. Dobbin, *Testing: Its Place in Education Today* (New York: Harper & Row, 1963), ch. 1; Julian C. Stanley, *Measurement in Today's Schools,* 4th ed. (Englewood Cliffs, N.J.: Prentice-Hall, 1964), ch. 2.

For an extended discussion of interest inventories and personality tests, instruments that will not be dealt with in this text, the following sources should be consulted: Anne Anastasi, *Psychological Testing;* Lee J. Cronbach, *Essentials of Psychological Testing,* 2nd ed. (New York: Harper & Row, 1960), chs. 14–16.

The following books present some of the current criticisms of various aspects of testing: Hillel Black, *They Shall Not Pass* (New York: William Morrow, 1963); Martin L. Gross, *The Brain Watchers* (New York: Random House, 1962); Banesh Hoffman, *The Tyranny of Testing* (New York: Crowell-Collier, 1962).

Chapter Two

Planning the Evaluation Process

The evaluation of pupil achievement may be defined as the process of determining how well pupils have attained specified instructional objectives. Evaluation, then, typically consists of a variety of techniques and procedures, including observations of pupil performance, grading of class exercises and homework assignments, and use of several different types of achievement tests. Because teachers use tests more than any other means for assessing pupil progress, they must have a clear understanding of the process of writing test items and selecting published examinations, and they must be proficient in using the results.

THE NEED FOR SPECIFIC BEHAVIORAL OBJECTIVES

Deciding how and when evaluations are to be made and what instruments are to be used depend on the instructional objectives being assessed. Consequently, any plan to appraise pupil achievement must start with clearly specified objectives. Unfortunately, although all teaching is directed toward some goal (even though it may be merely "keeping the students orderly for this class period" or "covering chapter three in the textbook"), objectives are seldom spelled out in such a way that they provide definite direction for evaluation.

In mentioning objectives, we are not talking about the general purposes of education such as those found in statements outlining the philosophy of a school system or in reports of persons or groups commissioned to define the "goals of education."[1] Nor are we

---

1. Examples of broad goals of this type may be found in: Educational Policies Commission, *The Purposes of Education in American Democracy* (Washing-

speaking of the overall goals for a given course. Such general and comprehensive statements are important in developing a total school program, but they must be broken down into specific details if they are to be used in determining pupil achievement. In order to evaluate what a pupil has learned in a given unit or an entire course, we must know the specific ways in which he should be able to exhibit that achievement. We must have statements of objectives describing what he should have learned in specific and limited units of instruction. We need statements that answer such questions as: "What should the pupil be able to do as a result of the instruction he received this week (or this month, or this day)?" The answers to such questions become statements that suggest the necessary evaluation procedures. Statements of instructional goals are sometimes referred to as "terminal behaviors" because they describe the behavior that a pupil should be able to exhibit at the termination of some period of instruction. Here they will be referred to as *specific behavioral objectives* or merely as *specific objectives*.

DERIVING SPECIFIC OBJECTIVES

Ideally, specific objectives will be spelled out in the course outlines or curriculum guides followed by the teacher. If a teacher basically wants to produce changes in pupils, his daily instruction should be guided by an exact knowledge of the nature of these desired changes. Unfortunately, the instructional objectives usually found in curriculum plans are neither specific nor behavioral. Even the better listings of objectives will include such statements as "The pupil will understand ———" or "He will have command of ———" without specifying exactly what he should be able to do to show that he "understands" or "has command of" the concept in question. The first step in evaluation is to translate the goals or objectives that have served as guides for teaching into a detailed listing of specific behavioral objectives that can direct evaluation efforts.[2]

ton, D.C.: American Council on Education, 1938); French, Will, and Associates, *Behavioral Goals of General Education in High School* (New York: Russell Sage Foundation, 1957); Harvard Committee on the Objectives of Education in a Free Society, *General Education in a Free Society* (Cambridge, Mass.: Harvard University Press, 1945).

2. The author has presented a rather detailed description of what is involved in the derivation of specific objectives in *Testing and Evaluation: An Introduction* (New York: Harcourt, Brace & World, 1961), ch. 2.

If statements of specific objectives are to be of maximum utility in evaluation, they should meet the following criteria:

1. *Objectives should be worded in terms of the pupil.* Because the evaluation is to determine what the pupil has achieved, objectives worded in terms of what the teacher does are of little value. Teacher-oriented objectives may cause the teacher to feel that education is completed when he has presented a lecture, whether or not his lecture actually taught the students anything. Objectives must be pupil centered.

2. *Objectives should be worded in terms of observable behavior.* Objectives specified in such words as "understand," "know," "appreciate," or "have command of" must be translated further if they are to provide a basis for evaluation. The evaluator must know exactly what behavior a student should be able to exhibit if he "understands," if he "knows," if he "appreciates." "Understand" may be translated into such behavioral terms as being able "to explain," "to give examples," or "to put in one's own words." "Knowing" implies being able to list, to supply terms, or to associate events with persons.

3. *Objectives should refer to the specific content to which the behavior is to apply.* If an objective is to have the specificity needed for evaluation, its exact content must be indicated. For example, the objective "the pupil will be able to spell correctly" makes no mention of the level of difficulty of the words intended; therefore, this objective would have different meanings for successive grade levels. If this objective is to provide a basis for evaluation, it must delineate the content, either by specifying the exact words to be spelled correctly or by describing their level of difficulty.

The task of defining specific behavioral objectives can be illustrated by examples taken from a recent curriculum development project.[3]

In developing a seventh-grade social studies unit on Africa, the curriculum committee started with such general goals as: (1) determine how geography has affected the politico-socioeconomic development; (2) understand the ever increasing importance of Africa in the world community. To make such goals meaningful for both

---

3. C. M. Lindvall, "The Importance of Specific Objectives in Curriculum Development," *Defining Educational Objectives* (Pittsburgh: University of Pittsburgh Press, 1964), pp. 14–16.

teaching and evaluation, it was necessary to decide what specific behavior a pupil should be able to exhibit if he had acquired the general abilities suggested by these statements. Therefore, the question that the curriculum developer or teacher raised at this point was: "What should I expect the pupil to be able to do if he has successfully determined how geography has affected the politico-socioeconomic development of Africa?" Answering this question resulted in such specific behavioral objectives as: The pupil should be able to (1) describe the geography of the various regions of Africa, (2) explain how geography has affected the economic development of at least one country from each major geographic division of Africa, and (3) explain how geography has affected the social and political development of those selected countries.

A similar question was raised concerning what a pupil should be able to do to show that he understood the ever increasing importance of Africa in the world community. The resulting specific objectives included such statements as: The pupil should be able to (1) list the contributions that African countries make to the world community, (2) describe some current world problems resulting from recent political changes in Africa, and (3) compare the influence that certain African nations had in the world community twenty-five years ago with their present influence.

Note that each of these specific objectives is behavioral, that it includes an action verb—*describe, explain, list, compare*—rather than a verb referring to a mental state—*understand, know, appreciate*. Stressing the need to translate objectives into behavioral terms does not mean that less importance is attached to an appreciation and deep understanding of what one has learned. It only means that these latter goals will be implicit in the terms that tell what specific behavior a pupil should be able to exhibit if he has achieved them.

PROCEDURES FOR ASSEMBLING SPECIFIC BEHAVIORAL OBJECTIVES AND IDEAS FOR EVALUATION

Planning for a test or for any evaluation process should not be left until the day before the pupils are to be evaluated. Specific behavioral objectives are a guide for teaching as well as for testing and should be outlined at the same time that lesson plans are being made. Each day's instruction is likely to be most effective if the teacher has a clear idea of what he expects pupils to be able to do as a result of their learning experiences on that day. Any valid procedure for evaluating achievement requires giving the student the opportunity to display the specific behavioral objectives outlined and then determining the extent to which he displays them.

If the instructional guides used by the teacher (a curriculum outline, a lesson plan, or an instruction manual) contain objectives worded in terms of pupil behavior, the first step in evaluation has already been completed. If, however (as is more typical), the instructional objectives are stated in general terms, the evaluator's first step will be to specify the behavioral objectives. He must go back over his instructional plans and materials and jot down the exact pupil abilities that his instruction is intended to produce. Only when he has such a list of specified abilities before him can he make any valid plans for pupil evaluation. This is the most important step in the entire evaluation process.

The task of identifying the important behavioral objectives is much easier in some subjects than in others. For subjects in which the instructional program expects students to develop skills by working various exercises, the desired behavior is usually evidenced in these exercises. In arithmetic, the student typically spends much of his time solving problems. The behavioral objectives toward which this study is directed are quite obvious in the homework problems. The same is true of other skill subjects such as reading, spelling, grammar, and composition.

In other areas, however, the task is not as easy. The working of exercises to develop specific skills and abilities is not usually part of the study of history, literature, or science. Here the student is expected to read and study a variety of materials in order to acquire certain understandings and appreciations and to be able to apply principles or generalizations. The behavioral abilities called for are not at all obvious and require much clear thinking. Unfortunately there are no rules or procedures that can simplify this task; the ability to specify behavioral objectives seems to depend on how well a teacher knows his subject.

One problem in assembling lists of educational objectives, particularly in the preparation of tests, is the possibility that such lists will overemphasize some types of abilities. For example, a teacher may tend to include too many objectives pertaining to a pupil's ability to display his knowledge, that is, his ability to list, to name, and to recall. In planning for teaching and testing, however, all the abilities that a pupil should be able to display with respect to any given subject-matter content should receive attention. The list might include objectives calling for the ability to explain, interpret, demonstrate, solve, analyze, organize, or plan, or for various other abilities more complex than those of rote learning.

USING THE TAXONOMY

In planning a list of objectives that will cover all the desired abilities, a teacher might obtain considerable help by consulting a listing of abilities such as the one found in *Taxonomy of Educational Objectives*.[4] The taxonomy,[5] developed by a group of university examiners, tries to construct a comprehensive outline of the cognitive abilities that could be acquired from any body of subject matter. The outline, which consists of six major categories, starts with the simplest ability, knowledge (defined as the ability to recall information), and builds up to abilities of much greater complexity. The taxonomy is outlined and described in great detail in Bloom's handbook, but the following major categories will illustrate its scope:

1.00 *Knowledge*
  1.10 Knowledge of Specifics.
    1.11 Knowledge of Terminology. Knowledge of the referents for specific symbols (verbal and nonverbal).
    1.12 Knowledge of Specific Facts. Knowledge of dates, events, persons, places, etc.
  1.20 Knowledge of Ways and Means of Dealing with Specifics.
    1.21 Knowledge of Conventions. Knowledge of characteristic ways of treating and presenting ideas and phenomena.

---

4. Benjamin S. Bloom, ed., *Taxonomy of Educational Objectives, Handbook I: Cognitive Domain* (New York: David McKay Co., 1956).
5. In discussing the taxonomy in this text, the reference will always be to *Handbook I: Cognitive Domain*. However, the reader should be aware of a companion volume, *Taxonomy of Educational Objectives, Handbook II: Affective Domain* by David Krathwohl, Benjamin S. Bloom, and Bertram B. Masia (New York: David McKay Co., 1964). The second handbook deals with objectives in the general realm of interests, attitudes, and other personality variables; because we will not be concerned with techniques for assessing such variables, it is not treated here.

1.22 Knowledge of Trends and Sequences. Knowledge of the processes, directions, and movements of phenomena with respect to time.

1.23 Knowledge of Classifications and Categories. Knowledge of the classes, sets, divisions, and arrangements that are regarded as fundamental for a given subject field, purpose, argument, or problem.

1.24 Knowledge of Criteria. Knowledge of the criteria by which facts, principles, and conduct are tested or judged.

1.25 Knowledge of Methodology. Knowledge of the methods of inquiry, techniques, and procedures employed in a particular subject field as well as those employed in investigating particular problems and phenomena.

1.30 Knowledge of the Universals and Abstractions in a Field.

1.31 Knowledge of Principles and Generalizations. Knowledge of particular abstractions that summarize observations of phenomena.

1.32 Knowledge of Theories and Structures. Knowledge of the body of principles and generalizations together with their interrelations which present a clear, rounded, and systematic view of a complex phenomenon, problem, or field.

2.00 *Comprehension*

2.10 Translation. Comprehension as evidenced by the care and accuracy with which the communication is paraphrased or rendered from one language or form of communication to another.

2.20 Interpretation. The explanation or summarization of a communication.

2.30 Extrapolation. The extension of trends or tendencies beyond the given data to determine implications, consequences, corollaries, effects, etc., that are in accordance with the conditions described in the original communication.

3.00 *Application* The use of abstractions in particular and concrete situations. The abstractions may be in the form of general ideas, rules of procedure, or generalized methods.

4.00 *Analysis*

4.10 Analysis of Elements. Identification of the elements included in a communication.

4.20 Analysis of Relationships. The connections and interactions between elements and parts of a communication.

4.30 Analysis of Organized Principles. The organization, systematic arrangement, and structure that hold the communication together.

5.00 *Synthesis*

5.10 Production of a Unique Communication. The development of a communication in which the writer or speaker attempts to convey ideas, feelings, or experiences to others.

5.20 Production of a Plan or Proposed Set of Operations. The development of a plan of work or the proposal of a plan of operations.

5.30 Derivation of a Set of Abstract Relations. The development of a set of abstract relations either to classify or to explain particular data or phenomena, or the deduction of propositions and relations from a set of basic propositions or symbolic representations.

6.00 *Evaluation*
6.10 Judgments in Terms of Internal Evidence. Evaluation of the accuracy of a communication from such evidence as logical accuracy, consistency, and other internal criteria.
6.20 Judgments in Terms of External Criteria. Evaluation of material with reference to selected or remembered criteria.

The handbook, in describing the various categories of the taxonomy, gives examples of objectives and specimen test items for each category, thus making the various parts of the outline much more understandable. However, the usefulness of the taxonomy does not depend on a complete understanding of every category and subcategory, nor does it depend on a capacity to make a definitive categorization of any given objective or test item (which has proved to be quite difficult even for those who have worked extensively with it). For the teacher, its most useful function is to call to his attention all the abilities that should be considered in assessing pupil achievement.

In outlining material for a test, this writer has found the first three categories—knowledge, comprehension, and application—to be the most useful.

Knowledge is concerned with a pupil's ability to recall terms, facts, rules, principles, and other generalizations—to name, list, state, describe, or define. The ability utilized is simple memory.

Comprehension is concerned with a pupil's ability to understand a given content to the extent that he can put it into his own words, summarize, or explain it. The abilities that would be found in objectives in this category include being able to translate, give examples, illustrate, interpret, summarize, or explain.

Application is concerned with a pupil's ability to use rules, methods, procedures, principles, and other types of generalization to produce or explain given consequences or to predict the result of some described situation. Objectives here would include being able to solve, predict, develop, explain, or apply.

Objectives that fall into the first three major categories of the taxonomy can be evaluated through the use of a variety of procedures, including objective tests.

Another category that should be given considerable attention in most evaluation programs is *synthesis*. The achievement of objectives in this category must, however, be assessed through such procedures as essay testing, assigning homework, observation of pupil performance, and other activities that actually require the pupil to develop, create, or produce something. Specific objectives are phrased in terms of the pupil's ability to develop a plan, to write a paper, to produce or to demonstrate something, or to show one of a number of other behaviors requiring the creation of something original.

Teachers and teacher-trainees can greatly improve the comprehensiveness of their lesson plans and their evaluation procedures by checking them against the objectives in these four categories.

USING A MATRIX

One useful way of outlining an instructional unit in order to reduce the possibility of overlooking the important goals of any particular subject content is to draw up a matrix, a table with content categories on one axis and ability categories on the other. An example is shown in Table 1 where a matrix is used to outline three units in a course in testing and evaluation such as the one being presented in this text. Four of the categories from the taxonomy, presented as sideheads, specify which abilities are of concern. This scheme will help a teacher consider whether there are objectives utilizing each of the four cognitive abilities in each content area.

The teacher should ask himself: "What facts or generalizations should the pupil know or remember from this unit? What things should he comprehend? What are the principles or procedures that he should be able to apply? What types of things should he be able to develop or synthesize?" This questioning should lead to greater comprehensiveness in both teaching and evaluating pupil achievement; however, it should not force the teacher to insert objectives in every cell of the matrix. The lack of objectives in certain cells in Table 1 suggests that there may be certain subject content units for which a given type of ability may not be important or appropriate. The matrix requires the teacher to consider whether a given type of ability is important in a given unit.

TABLE 1

A MATRIX SHOWING INSTRUCTIONAL OBJECTIVES FOR THREE
UNITS IN A COURSE IN TESTING AND EVALUATION

Cognitive abilities involved	Content units		
	Specifying objectives	Criteria for evaluation instruments	Constructing tests
Knowledge	Can list sources of objectives	Can list criteria used in judging evaluation instruments	Can list various types of tests
	Can state criteria for specific objectives		Can state rules and suggestions for constructing tests and test items
Comprehension	Can state criteria in own words	Can state criteria in own words	
		Can give examples of criteria	
Application	Can use criteria to state specific objectives	Can use criteria to select best procedure for a given purpose	Can use suggestions to construct test items
Synthesis	Can develop an outline of overall goals and specific objectives for a unit		Can develop valid and effective tests

CHOOSING THE EVALUATION PROCEDURE

When a teacher has an outline showing the specific behavioral objectives for a given unit of instruction, he is then in a position to select the most appropriate methods of evaluation for his needs. He should be guided by certain criteria that define the important qualities in any evaluation procedure. These criteria will be introduced and discussed in relatively nontechnical terms in this chapter. The discussion will be sufficient to enable the teacher to decide what is the best procedure for assessing classroom achievement. Some of these criteria will be presented in greater depth at later points in the text where a more technical discussion is necessary.

Validity. Any procedure for obtaining information about students is valid to the extent that it actually provides the desired information. In the evaluation of pupil achievement, the information desired is the degree to which pupils have achieved the specified instructional objectives. The important question on the validity of any procedure for assessing pupil achievement is, then, whether it provides evidence of the extent to which pupils are able to exhibit the specific behavior described in the objectives. Validity is, of course, the most important quality to be sought in an evaluation procedure, for if that procedure does not give us the information we are seeking, it will be of little value.

The need for validity, then, suggests the first consideration in selecting an appropriate procedure—it should be one stipulated by the behavior described in the objective. If the objective states that the pupil should be able to list, name, or define, we should give him an opportunity to do this, either orally or in writing. If he is expected to explain, describe, translate, or interpret, he should have a chance to do these things. In all these instances the evaluation procedure could be an oral quiz, an essay examination, or, in some instances, an objective test. If a specific objective states that the pupil should be able to perform certain feats or demonstrate certain skills, evaluation could be made through observation of pupil performance. The important point is that we must give the pupil the opportunity to display the ability described in the specific objectives and then assess the extent to which he has done this.

Another point to emphasize is that no instrument or procedure is valid in and of itself. A procedure may be valid in one situation for a given purpose and quite invalid in another situation or for another purpose. Validity also depends on how a procedure is applied and how the resulting pupil performance is assessed. We are concerned with the results, and in selecting the proper procedure we are taking only the first step toward validity.

In many situations the teacher will employ the most direct and valid procedure for assessing a particular type of pupil achievement; however, he may also wish to supplement this evaluation by using another procedure that is less obviously valid but which has certain qualities that are lacking in the first procedure. For example, assume that an objective states that the pupil should, after reading data presented in the form of graphs, be able to explain how several countries differ in such characteristics as population, amount of rainfall, agricultural exports, and per capita wealth. The direct way to evaluate this objective would be to give the pupil graphic data on the given countries and ask him to write an explanation of how they differ. This is a valuable procedure and would undoubtedly be used. However, if the teacher relied solely on this procedure, he might be troubled by the fact that his entire assessment of the pupils' achievement of this objective depended upon his own subjective judgment of each pupil's explanation. The teacher might therefore choose to supplement his evaluation obtained through this essay examination by also making use of some objective test items. For example, he might present the students with appropriate tabular data and then use multiple-choice questions requiring them to select the best explanations of what the tables show. Here the objective would not be evaluated directly because the students would not be required "to explain," but only "to select the best explanation." However, there is a close connection between these two abilities, and the greater objectivity and reliability of the second procedure could make the information it provided a very useful supplement to that yielded by the more direct procedure.

There are additional reasons why the problem of selecting an evaluation procedure is not always settled by relying solely on the obvious method suggested by the behavioral objective. In some situations the obvious method may not produce the comprehensive assessment needed. Let us assume that an objective states that a pupil will use correct punctuation in his writing. The direct and most obviously valid procedure for evaluating this ability is to require the student to submit a number of written assignments and to grade each of these for punctuation. However, a given pupil may turn in a number of such assignments yet never need to use several kinds of punctuation that he is supposed to have mastered. To overcome this difficulty the teacher might employ as a supplementary evaluation procedure a test requiring the pupil to punctuate correctly a number of given sentences and paragraphs. This second procedure could be made comprehensive enough to cover all types of punctuation that had been studied, thus making it a useful and necessary supplement to the more direct procedure.

These examples of situations where the most valid evaluation procedure is not necessarily entirely sufficient for determining pupil achievement suggest that although validity is the most important quality to be sought, additional qualities must be considered in planning evaluation. We will now turn to a consideration of some of these other criteria.

Reliability. A data-gathering procedure is reliable to the extent that it will produce consistent results in assessing the same thing. If we use a reading-readiness test to determine whether a first-grade pupil is ready to profit from formal instruction in reading, we must know that, no matter whether we give him the test in the morning, in the afternoon, or tomorrow, we will get essentially the same results. If the test cannot produce results that are consistent in this sense, we will not know when to apply it to get the actual measure of the pupil's readiness. It is obvious that reliability is important in any procedure for obtaining information about pupils.

As with validity, the reliability of a procedure is dependent on other things in addition to the particular test or device being used. It depends on the conditions under which it is administered, on the nature of the quality being measured, and on the way in which results are scored or assessed. All these things must be taken into consideration in trying to ensure adequate reliability.

Reliability is also a matter of degree. No procedure is absolutely reliable. If we use a weight scale to measure the weights of pupils, there is a certain degree of unreliability because of the lack of perfect accuracy in reading the dial, differences in the weights of clothing worn by the pupils, and minor inconsistencies in the operation of the scale itself. Similarly, with tests and other evaluation procedures we recognize that the results will not be perfectly reliable; our goal is to secure the most reliable results possible.

Among various evaluation procedures, some are generally more reliable than others. If, for example, we use oral quizzing of the class as a method of assessing achievement, we should recognize certain sources of unreliability. Typically, we cannot ask many questions of any one student, so we are forced to evaluate each student on the basis of a very limited sample of responses. It is quite possible that if a given student had been asked to respond to different questions, the adequacy of his answers might have been quite different. Thus, results from the oral quiz are generally unreliable. A written examination in which each student responds to a relatively large number of questions should produce more reliable results. Another reason for the unreliability of the oral quiz s that all responses are subjectively graded by the teacher. To the extent that a teacher's moods and perceptions change, a given response might be graded in one way at one time and quite differently at another. This same subjectivity in grading also means that use of essay examinations and homework assignments as a basis for evaluation produces results less reliable than those obtained through more objective procedures.

Of course, the fact that these subjective procedures are somewhat less reliable than desirable does not mean that they should not be used. In many cases they are necessary because of their high validity for a specific purpose. However, the results of subjective evaluation might well be checked by the use of more objective procedures.

Objectivity. Objectivity, when used in connection with evaluation devices, may be defined as the extent to which an assessment is independent of the subjective judgment of the evaluator. In the discussion of reliability, it was pointed out that a lack of objectivity in scoring could produce inconsistent and unreliable results. For this reason objectivity is often sought as a means for improving the reliability of an evaluation.

Objectivity is also desirable for another reason. An objective assessment is more likely to be acceptable to the person whose work is being evaluated. Results from subjective procedures may be taken by the student as merely representing the biased opinion of the teacher and therefore as something to be rejected. Results from the use of objective methods may be taken less as personal judgments and more as independent and unbiased evaluations.

On the other hand, there is evidence that many pupils are interested in the subjective judgment of the teacher. They feel that he is an expert in his field and that his judgment, based on a more comprehensive understanding of the subject, may be more meaningful than the result produced by an objective device. Objectivity can be of considerable importance and should be sought in many types of evaluation, but other types of performance that must be assessed are so complex that they should be evaluated only through subjective procedures.

Comprehensiveness. Most of us have been students in classroom situations where the teacher was quizzing students orally and we fervently hoped we would be asked questions we knew the answers to. We recognized that there were certain aspects of the lesson we had not mastered but knew that, if we could make a good showing in our responses to the few questions we were given, we might convince the teacher that we were "A" students. Unfortunately, however, we were sometimes asked questions we could not answer and, hence, gave the teacher the exactly opposite impression.

When we look at this situation from the teacher's point of view, we can understand how this lack of comprehensiveness in assessing the achievement of any one pupil can yield misleading information. As we mentioned previously, the extent to which the teacher takes a pupil's responses to one or a few questions as representing his command of all the questions asked will produce results of low reliability. If the teacher does not make this assumption, if he takes a pupil's answer to a particular question as showing only his command of that particular point, then the information obtained concerning any particular student is extremely limited.

A concern for comprehensiveness should be a part of the planning for any evaluation. The oral quiz is not the only type of test that is limited in this respect; another test may be confined to topics that can be tested most easily. Teachers frequently become so stereotyped in their behavior that they continually ask the same type of essay questions or habitually use objective items that measure only one type of ability.

The carefully planned evaluation program will start with a detailed outline of all of the objectives to be covered and then will ensure that all students are evaluated accordingly. Comprehensiveness should be a very conscious goal, and it can be achieved only through careful planning.

Other Considerations.   The four criteria discussed in the preceding sections are basic to the planning of any evaluation process. Certainly the validity and reliability of the results must be uppermost in the mind of the teacher as he plans his procedures for assessing achievement and as he develops the needed instruments. Objectivity and comprehensiveness, although slightly less central in importance, also merit attention.

In addition to these basic criteria, several other considerations, although of relatively minor importance, will play a part in determining what evaluation procedures will be used.

EASE OF CONSTRUCTION AND SCORING. Some instruments, such as check lists, rating scales, and objective-type tests, may be relatively more difficult to construct than less formal procedures. However, this difficulty may be balanced by the greater ease in scoring. The teacher may wish to give these two aspects of ease of use some thought in selecting a procedure.

ECONOMY OF CLASS TIME. Certain techniques of evaluation may require considerable class time. For example, personal interviews could be quite time-consuming. In considering the use of interviews, the teacher must decide whether it would represent the most efficient use of class time. Other procedures, such as written tests, are generally more efficient because all pupils are being examined at the same time.

ECONOMY OF TEACHER TIME. Different evaluation procedures will take different amounts of a teacher's time. If lengthy term papers are used as a major means of assessing achievement, careful checking of these papers should take considerable time. Another time-consuming procedure is the compiling and analyzing of anecdotal records on each student. In many cases the investment of major blocks of a teacher's time in these types of evaluation procedures may represent the very best use of his time. However, the teacher himself must always decide how his time can best be spent.

SUMMARY

Education is a process of producing desired changes in the behavior of the learner. If education is to be effective, frequent assessments must be made of the extent to which the desired behavioral changes have been produced. This evaluation of pupil achievement must be based on clearly defined instructional objectives that will be most helpful in guiding both evaluation and instruction if they (1) are worded in terms of the pupil, (2) are worded in terms of observable behavior, and (3) refer to the specific content of the behavior. In formulating the specific objectives for a course or for a unit of instruction, the teacher should make certain that they cover various types of abilities. Aid in achieving this coverage may be obtained by using a listing of types of abilities such as the one found in *Taxonomy of Educational Objectives.*

Objectives worded in specific behavioral terms are essential in making certain that an evaluation procedure provides direct evidence of pupil achievement of a desired ability. This quality of *validity* is the major criterion to be considered in developing or selecting a test or other evaluation device. Other important criteria include *reliability, objectivity, comprehensiveness,* and *usability.*

Suggestions for Class Discussion and Further Investigation

1. Develop a matrix of objectives, such as the one presented in this chapter, for some course or unit of study that is of interest to you. Make certain that all objectives are stated in terms of pupil behaviors.
2. In the section on deriving specific objectives, certain action verbs such as *describe, explain, list,* and *compare* were suggested as examples of the types of behavioral abilities that should be found in statements of specific objectives. For each of the six major taxonomy categories develop a list of comparable action verbs that would be appropriate for objectives falling into a particular category.
3. Suggestions 1 and 2 in chapter one asked you to list the weaknesses of an evaluation procedure that relies solely on class discussion and observation. Re-examine each such objection or weakness and determine if it is a weakness in validity, reliability, objectivity, or another criterion considered desirable in an evaluation procedure or instrument.
4. Secure copies of published achievement tests. For each item in the tests decide in which taxonomy category the ability being measured would fall.

Suggestions for Further Reading

For an excellent summary and discussion of various points of view on the general goals of American education, the student is referred to Paul Woodring, *Introduction to American Education* (New York: Harcourt, Brace & World, 1965), ch. 3.

Clear and detailed explanations of what is meant by specification of instructional objectives is found in the following sources: Robert M. Gagne, *The Conditions of Learning* (New York: Holt, Rinehart and Winston, 1965), ch. 9; Robert F. Mager,

Preparing Objectives for Programmed Instruction (San Francisco: Fearon Publishers, 1962).

Rather complete discussions of the task required in deriving specific behavioral objectives from broad goals of education (including examples) will be found in the following sources: Norman E. Gronlund, *Measurement and Evaluation in Teaching* (New York: Macmillan, 1965), ch. 2; E. F. Lindquist, ed., *Educational Measurement* (Washington, D.C.: American Council on Education, 1951), ch. 5; R. Murray Thomas, *Judging Student Progress* (New York: David McKay Co., 1954), ch. 2.

The various criteria that must be considered in assessing an evaluation instrument are discussed at some length in: Julian C. Stanley, *Measurement in Today's Schools,* 4th ed. (Englewood Cliffs, N.J.: Prentice-Hall, 1964), ch. 5; Lee J. Cronbach, *Essentials of Psychological Testing,* 2nd ed. (New York: Harper & Row, 1960), chs. 5–6.

Chapter Three

Principles of
Achievement Test Construction

The evaluation device used most frequently by the majority of teachers is undoubtedly the teacher-made test; therefore, it is essential that the beginning teacher be skilled in the development and use of such devices. Fortunately, the matter of how to develop and use classroom tests has received considerable attention in past years, and many useful criteria and suggestions have been prepared. The teacher who makes conscientious use of what is available in this area can greatly improve the quality of his tests.

THE ROLE OF TEACHER-MADE TESTS

Good classroom tests provide an efficient means for determining pupil ability and achievement. Carefully developed tests can rate quite high on all the criteria discussed in chapter two. The use of tests in evaluation is an *economical use of class time* because all pupils are giving information about themselves simultaneously. It is also possible to obtain a relatively *comprehensive* assessment of pupil achievement. If the test is carefully planned and constructed, it can also rate high on the key criteria of *validity* and *reliability*. These desirable qualities plus its relative *simplicity in use* have made the classroom test one of the most effective tools available to the teacher.

TYPES OF TEACHER-MADE TESTS

The types of test questions most frequently used by teachers can be categorized as follows:

1. Essay questions.
2. Completion or supply-type items.
3. Selection-type items.
   a. True-false.
   b. Multiple-choice.
   c. Matching.

Obviously the item types vary in the degree to which the examinee must supply the answer rather than make a selection among given alternatives and also in the degree to which the items can be scored objectively. In both the essay and completion types the student must provide the answer; however, in the completion items he supplies only one or a few words while in the essay he must provide everything.

Completion items are frequently classed with selection-type items, and all are referred to as objective-type items. Here the word "objective" means that the scoring can be done independently of the subjective judgment of the scorer. The selection-type items can, of course, be scored in a completely objective manner. Once a scoring key has been developed, the scorer does not need to make any subjective decisions, and scoring can be done just as effectively by a clerk or a machine as by the teacher. However, with completion or supply-type items this is not true. Here a scoring key will be developed and used, but it can be anticipated that students will supply some answers not listed on the scoring key that will have to be accepted as correct. Decisions in such situations will require the subjective judgment of the teacher. Hence, completion-type items are not altogether objective and probably should not be classed with selection-type items.

ESSAY QUESTIONS

The most subjective type of test item to score is the essay question. In an essay test the examinee must construct sentences, paragraphs, and written passages of varying length to demonstrate that he has the ability being tested. The length of the required responses may vary from a single sentence, which might be sufficient in a second-grade test, to a lengthy composition requiring a day or more to complete in a comprehensive examination for some type of professional certification. The essential characteristic of the essay item is that it requires the examinee to write at least one sentence and that the answer must be assessed subjectively by the teacher or other authority on the content.

Using the Essay Question.   The essay question should be used only when it has been judged the most valid and efficient procedure for a given purpose. The teacher should not use it merely because he has developed the habit of relying exclusively on it or because it seems to be the simplest type of test to construct. The essay test can be extremely valid for evaluating certain kinds of objectives and may be helpful in promoting desirable study and planning by students. Also, it gives the examinee valuable practice in organizing his ideas and trying to express them effectively. On the other hand, the typical unreliability of the scores obtained and the relative inefficiency in the use of testing time suggest that the essay test should not be chosen if some more objective procedure is equally valid.

If the purpose of the test is to determine the extent to which pupils have acquired certain knowledge, supply-type items or selection-type items will usually prove more effective than essay questions. Essay examinations should be used to evaluate more complex abilities such as a student's competence to organize ideas, develop an argument, make comparisons, interpret information, and display other abilities involving original written verbal expression, and, when the intended objectives are stated in terms of such abilities, the essay test should be given first consideration.

Constructing the Essay Question.   If an essay test is to be useful for measuring the desired abilities, considerable care must be taken in developing the questions. These questions should not be dashed off hurriedly on the day of the test but should be planned well in advance so that they can be re-examined and edited before they are used.

An essay item must clearly specify the desired response. If the examinee in writing his answer to an item does not exhibit the desired ability because he does not understand the question, then his low score represents invalid information about his achievement. To avoid this situation each essay question should be worded so clearly and specifically that all pupils will interpret it correctly.

A common mistake in writing essay items is to make the statements too general. Consider, for example, a question that might be used with some of the content of this chapter: "Discuss the objective-type test." With the item worded in these broad terms, different examinees will probably concentrate on different aspects of the topic. One student might discuss the kinds of items that are usually considered objective and offer suggestions for the construction of each. Another might describe the problems of using this type of test to measure different abilities and compare it with the essay examination. Still another might explain how objective-type tests rate with respect to the various qualities that are generally sought in an evaluation device. If the teacher had one of these approaches in mind and penalized those students who did not use it, he would be making the judgment that failure to discuss this topic indicated lack of mastery of it; his judgment might not be valid.

To avoid ambiguity and to be certain of obtaining the same type of information about all examinees, the above question should be rephrased in more specific terms. One example might be: "Explain why certain kinds of test items are called 'objective.' Describe completion and multiple-choice items and compare their objectivity." Note that this essay item, although much more restricted in what it requests from the student, is necessarily much longer than the previous, more general, statement.

The revised form of our test question may be criticized because it does not require the student to display his knowledge of other aspects of the topic; it is too restricted in the abilities that it samples. However, if greater sampling is desired, the student should be asked to respond to several relatively brief, specific items rather than to one broad, vague question.

Scoring Essay Examinations.   Because the major weakness of the essay examination lies in the subjectivity and possible unreliability of the scoring procedures, the scoring must be carefully planned. The following steps can be helpful.

1. Develop a scoring key. Although this key will be somewhat different from that used with an objective-type test and cannot be applied with as much objectivity, it is essential for meaningful scoring. The key typically consists of an outline of the ideal answer and indicates the number of points that are to be awarded to the

student for including each element in the outline. For example, the key for scoring the essay question on objective-type test items might be outlined as follows:

1. Definition of objective-type item   2 points
2. Meaning of objectivity   2 points
3. The completion-type item
   a. Description   2 points
   b. Degree of objectivity   2 points
4. The multiple-choice item
   a. Description   2 points
   b. Degree of objectivity   2 points
5. Comparison of completion and multiple-choice   4 points

The arbitrary decision has been made that each of the first six elements in the outline is worth 2 points, while the final element is worth 4. The assignment of points to each element is made by the teacher on the basis of his judgment of the relative importance of each specific ability. Usually, however, the simpler the weighting system, the more reliable the results will be. In using the above key, the teacher will first look for the examinee's definition of an objective-type item. If it is stated in an essentially correct form, the answer will earn 2 points. If the definition is only partially correct, the answer may earn only 1 point. If the answer does not contain a definition, or if the given definition is totally incorrect, no points will be awarded. The teacher then goes on to score each element in the same manner. Note that the task of comparing completion and multiple-choice items has been judged to be of greater importance than any other single element in the answer and that here the scorer can award anything from 0 to 4 points. It should also be noted that if the teacher felt there were certain definite matters that should be included in the comparison, these could be listed as subcategories under element 5 and each could be assigned some part of the total 4 points.

2. If the essay examination consists of several items, score the answers to the first item on all papers; then go on to score the second item, and so on. This procedure will increase the probability that for any given item the same standards will be used on all papers. It should also be helpful in reducing the "halo effect," or the probability that the scorer's judgment of the value of an answer

to one item on a pupil's test paper will be influenced by his overall impression of the paper.

3. If possible, score each paper without looking to see the name of the examinee. This is another effort to reduce the "halo effect." If the scorer does not know whose paper he is grading, his previous general impressions of the student cannot influence the score he assigns. Scoring will then be on the basis of the present written answer alone.

4. During the process of scoring, periodically recheck some of the papers that were scored earlier. This review should improve the chances that a relatively uniform standard will be used for all papers.

COMPLETION OR SUPPLY-TYPE QUESTIONS

Completion items are statements with one or more missing words that must be provided by the examinee. The following items are simple examples of this form:

During the Civil War, the commander of the Army of Northern Virginia was General _____.
The chemical symbol for mercury is _____.

Another form of this item is a question that can be answered with one or a few words. The items given above can easily be reworded in question form:

Who was the commander of the Army of Northern Virginia during the Civil War? _____
What is the chemical symbol for mercury? _____

In either form, the essential features of this kind of item are that the answers consist of only one or two words and that these words must be supplied by the examinee rather than selected from a list of available alternatives.

Using the Completion Question. Completion items are useful in evaluating a variety of educational objectives. They are appropriate whenever an objective specifies that the pupil should be able to name, list, or supply the answer. When the pupil is expected to have memorized certain terms, names of persons, dates, or symbols, the completion or supply-type item will probably be the most valid and most effective form of test question to use.

This kind of item has the advantage of being relatively easy to construct, particularly when compared with multiple-choice and matching items, since it does not require a list of plausible distracters. Another of its strengths is that it provides little opportunity for guessing; either the examinee can supply the answer or he cannot. He has no chance to guess from among provided alternatives.

As has already been mentioned, this form of item lacks complete objectivity. Because the person constructing the scoring key can seldom anticipate all the possible correct answers that students might insert, the scorer will frequently be required to make subjective decisions. Another weakness of the completion or supply-type item is that too much reliance on it may lead to an overemphasis on memorization of factual information. Although rote learning is essential in most subject-matter areas, it is only one ability and must not be emphasized to the neglect of other, more complex abilities.

Constructing the Completion Question. The following suggestions have been found to be helpful in preparing effective completion items.

1. Word each item so specifically that the desired answer is the only one possible. Consider the following:

World War II ended in _____.

A number of different expressions ("Japan," "victory," "1945") could be used to complete this statement correctly. If the item is intended to test whether the examinee knows the year in which the war ended, it should be worded:

World War II ended in the year _____.

This more specific statement rules out such answers as "Japan" and "victory."

2. Do not insert more than one or two blanks in any completion item. The addition of more typically results in a "butchered" sen-

tence that could be answered correctly with a variety of combinations; for example:

The _____ type of test item is usually more _____ than the _____ type.

Of course, many different words could be used to complete this statement correctly, but each combination of words yields a sentence with a different meaning. A better item would be:

The supply-type of test item is usually graded more objectively than the _____ type.

---

3. Word the statement so that the blank is near the end of the sentence. This practice ensures more efficient testing because the examinee will have the major idea of the statement in mind before he has to think of the element he must supply; the informed examinee will then have to read the item only once. If the blank is near the beginning of the sentence, he will have to read the item once to grasp the idea and then again to see if his answer is correct. One advantage of using the question form in supply-type items is that the blank necessarily appears at the end.

4. Do not use statements copied from a textbook or other lesson source. A temptation in constructing completion items is to select key sentences from a textbook and form test items merely by putting blanks in place of certain words. There are at least two important reasons for avoiding this practice. First, key sentences often are not specific enough to constitute good items. That is, the sentence may make sense only in context and by itself may not contain all the words necessary to make it clear and specific. Second, if students know that a teacher makes liberal use of sentences copied directly from the textbook, their study will tend to be essentially memorization. When material is taken from a printed source, it should be reworded so that memory alone will not be sufficient to enable the pupil to do well on the test.

5. In most cases the question form is more effective than the incomplete statement because (1) the question form tends to be more specific, (2) the blank is at the end of the item, (3) there is no chance of producing a "butchered" sentence, and (4) there is less likelihood that a question can be copied verbatim from a printed text.

TRUE-FALSE QUESTIONS

In these items the examinee must decide whether a given statement is true or false. For example, the items used to illustrate the completion form could be reworded as:

The commander of the Army of Northern Virginia during the Civil War was General Robert E. Lee.	
The chemical symbol for mercury is Au.	T Ⓕ

Variations in this two-alternative item include the use of such word pairs as "yes-no," "right-wrong," or "correct-incorrect" as the responses. Another variation is the "true-false with correction" item. In this latter type, the examinee is instructed to mark each item either true or false *and* to correct each false statement. In one procedure, the student is told to cross out that part of an item which makes it false and to write in the words necessary to make it true. In another procedure, each of the items has a key word underlined, and for each false statement the student is to substitute another word for the one underlined to make the statement true. The second procedure is preferable to the first because it makes scoring more manageable and reliable.

In still another variation, Robert L. Ebel[1] suggests that, instead of being asked to choose from only two alternatives, the examinee should be asked to select from five: (1) probably true, (2) possibly true, (3) I have no idea, (4) possibly false, (5) probably false. Ebel discusses several plans for giving the different responses varying weights.

Using the True-False Question.   The true-false item should probably be used less frequently than it is because it is generally regarded as the weakest of the objective items. In most cases a teacher's evaluation of his students will be better if he employs the multiple-choice rather than the true-false item. However, use of the true-false or other type of two-response item may be justified where there are obviously only two alternatives and where the attempt

---

1. *Measuring Educational Achievement* (Englewood Cliffs, N.J.: Prentice-Hall, 1965), pp. 130–33.

to develop a multiple-choice item would result in some highly implausible distracters.

A major weakness of the true-false item is of course the fact that if the pupil is totally uninformed about a given item and has to make a blind guess, he still has a 50 percent chance of supplying the correct answer. Thus scores from true-false tests are typically less reliable than are scores from multiple-choice tests. The high probability of guessing correctly often results in poor study habits. In addition, a pupil answering test items as true when actually they are false may retain this incorrect information.

For the pupil one advantage of the true-false item is economy of time; examinees typically can answer more items of this type than of other types in a given amount of time. When it is essential that the maximum amount of material be covered in a limited amount of time, the true-false test could be the most efficient procedure. Completely objective scoring is, of course, another advantage of this type of item.

Some teachers act on the assumption that an additional advantage of the true-false item is ease of construction. That is, they use this form because they find they can write a series of items rather quickly. This assumption is false, and the poor test items that usually result from it constitute a major reason why many teacher-made tests are of such poor quality: the construction of good true-false items actually requires careful planning and considerable time.

Constructing the True-False Question. The teacher who uses true-false items should find the following suggestions helpful for improving the quality of his tests.

1. Construct statements that are definitely true or definitely false. This is important both for achieving valid and reliable test results and for avoiding the possibility that the examinee may acquire some incorrect ideas from taking the test. The teacher will be aided in the construction of unambiguous test items if he

   a. uses relatively short statements.

   b. uses language that is as exact as possible. For example, where feasible, he should use quantitative rather than qualitative terms.

   c. avoids the use of complex sentences containing more than one major idea; such sentences may yield incorrect information about a student's knowledge. Consider the following item, for example:

The Ohio and Mississippi rivers meet at Cairo, Illinois, to form the Missouri River.   T (F)

A student may mark this item false because he thinks that the Ohio River does not join the Mississippi at Cairo. His inadvertently correct response, however, would be taken to mean that he knows that when the Ohio joins the Mississippi at Cairo, the combined rivers continue as the Mississippi. The incorporation of two major facts has resulted in incorrect information concerning this pupil's knowledge.

   d. attributes opinions or attitudes used as item content to some particular source so that the examinee knows the teacher is not asking for personal opinion. Items of this type might start with such qualifying phrases as "From the point of view of the writer of our textbook" or "In the opinion of most authorities in this field."

2. Avoid giving the examinee irrelevant verbal clues from the consistent use of certain words in true items and certain others in false items. Strongly worded items containing *all, always, definitely, never,* and *undoubtedly,* are usually false. Statements with such indefinite qualifying words as *frequently, may, most, should,* and *some* are typically true. The teacher should be alert to this possibility of giving away answers and should edit his items to eliminate these irrelevant clues.

3. Do not copy sentences from textbooks or other printed lesson source materials. A sentence may be entirely true when it is read within context, but, because of a lack of explanation and clarification, it may not be true when it stands alone in a test item. Furthermore, the consistent practice of copying test items from printed lesson materials encourages undesirable rote learning.

4. Do not be tempted to simplify scoring by arranging the items so that there is some easily memorized repetitive pattern to the correct responses (TFFTFF or TFFTTF, for example). Students soon discover such patterns and thus invalidate the test results. For a similar reason, it is best to avoid the practice of consistently having many more true responses than false or many more false responses than true.

MULTIPLE-CHOICE QUESTIONS

A multiple-choice item consists of a *stem* plus two or more *alternatives,* one of which meets the requirement demanded by the stem. The item stem is an incomplete statement, and the alternative responses are possible endings for it:

_____ 1. Specific instructional objectives are most useful to the test developer if they are stated in terms of
    a. the specific content covered.
    b. the desired pupil behavior.
    c. the teaching activities to be carried out.
    d. what the pupil should know.

In another frequently used form, the item stem is worded as a question for which the examinee is to select the correct answer:

_____ 2. Which one of the following types of test item can be scored most objectively?
    a. True-false
    b. Essay
    c. Completion

Although these are the most commonly used, there are many other forms possible. For example, the stem may be a word followed by several pictures from which the examinee is to select the one best described by the word. The reverse is also frequently employed —the item stem is a picture, and the alternatives are words, only one of which fits the picture.

The number of possible forms that effective multiple-choice items may take is limited only by the test constructor's imagination. The beginning teacher can get many ideas by examining items on the better published tests.

Using the Multiple-Choice Question. The multiple-choice question is generally considered to be the most useful of the objective-type items. Tests using it are usually more reliable than those containing other types because (1) they can be scored on a completely objective basis, and (2) providing several alternatives for each item reduces the role that guessing plays in determining the examinee's score. Furthermore, multiple-choice items can be used to evaluate a greater variety of abilities than can the other items. The next chapter will provide examples of this diversity. A multiple-choice item tests the ability to make fine discriminations by asking the pupil to select "the most important reason," "the principal cause," or "the best explanation."

The assertion that the multiple-choice item is generally superior to other forms is supported by the fact that almost all items on most published tests are of this form. Publishers have found that questions originally phrased as completion or true-false items can be made more effective by rewording them as multiple-choice. Most classroom teachers will find the same to be true concerning their own tests, once they have gained some mastery of the steps in test construction. They should find that their testing will improve if they make greater use of multiple-choice items and place less reliance on true-false and completion questions.

Constructing the Multiple-Choice Question. The following suggestions may be useful for writing effective multiple-choice items.

1. Write as many items as possible in question form. In most cases a question makes the best item stem because it is worded specifically and deals with only one important idea. Rendering a statement in question form also reduces the possibility that the item will be copied directly from a textbook. If the incomplete-statement form seems necessary, test the clarity and specificity of the stem by determining whether the statement contains all the information that would be included in the corresponding question.

2. Include at least three alternatives for every stem. A multiple-choice item with only two alternatives allows a 50 percent chance that a blind guess will be correct, thus giving no advantage over a true-false item. To minimize the probability that a pupil will guess the correct answer, provide four or five alternatives if possible.

3. Make certain that all the incorrect alternatives, the *distracters,* are plausible enough so that none can be dismissed as absurd by an examinee who does not really know the correct answer.

4. If the item stem is a statement, make certain that all distracters provide grammatically correct endings to the sentence. Sometimes, in his haste to add distracters, a teacher words some of the listed alternatives so poorly that they can be dismissed simply because they do not form a sentence when read with the stem. A simple example is an item stem that obviously requires a singular response accompanied by plural distracters.

5. Make the responses as short as feasible by including in the

item stem any words that would otherwise be unnecessarily repeated in each response. A poor item would be

---

1. Columbus' ships
   a. were named the Godspeed, the Discovery, and the Susan Constant.
   b. were named the Niña, the Pinta, and the Santa María.
   c. were named the María, the Carla, and the Piñata.

The item could be improved simply by including "were named" in the stem.

6. Do not consistently avoid any one of the response positions as the place for the correct answer. For example, do not get into the habit of never putting the correct response in the first position.

7. Try to make all the responses approximately the same length. Beginners in test construction frequently find that their correct answers are consistently longer than the distracters. This provides the examinee with an irrelevant clue to the correct answer.

8. The responses "none of the above" or "not given" may be useful in items with only one possible answer, as in problems involving numerical computation. They should not be used in a "best answer" type of item. When this option is presented, care should be taken to make certain that it fits grammatically with the stem.

9. The response "all the above" should seldom be used by a beginning item-writer. If items requiring this response are not worded with great care, they can cause undesirable confusion for the examinee.

10. Use consistent and correct punctuation. Do not place any punctuation at the end of the incomplete-statement stem unless the sentence requires it. Each response should start with a lower-case letter (unless it is a proper name or other word requiring capitalization) and end with a period or other appropriate terminal punctuation. When the question form is used, the stem should end with a question mark, and each response should start with a capital letter. (See the examples on page 41.)

MATCHING QUESTIONS

A matching exercise consists of two lists of words, phrases, pictures, or other symbols and a set of instructions explaining the basis on which the examinee is to match an item in the first list with an item in the second list. For example:

In the lefthand column below are titles given to some of the founders of our nation. For each title choose a name from the righthand column and place the letter identifying it on the line preceding the number of the title. Each item in the righthand column may be used once, more than once, or not at all.

_____ 1. Father of the Constitution	a. Edmund Randolph
_____ 2. First Secretary of the Treasury	b. James Madison
_____ 3. Proposer of the Virginia Plan	c. John Jay
_____ 4. Republican proponent of agrarian democracy	d. Alexander Hamilton
	e. Thomas Jefferson
_____ 5. Leader of the Federalists	
_____ 6. First Chief Justice of the Supreme Court	

In a matching exercise, the elements of the list that is read first are referred to as *premises,* and the elements in the other list are called *responses.* In the above example, the premises appear in a lefthand column, but in some cases the premises may be placed above or below the responses.

A matching exercise may be thought of as a set of multiple-choice items in which all the stems have the same options. The example exercise above has six scoring units. That is, the examinee receives one point for each premise for which he selects the correct response. Here there are more premises than responses, but it is also possible to have more responses than premises or to make the two lists equal in length.

Using the Matching Question.   As its name suggests, this type of test item evaluates a pupil's ability to match or associate related objects or ideas. Many school subjects require that a pupil be able to associate terms with definitions, names of places with locations, ideas or procedures with their uses, or names of persons with events. Where there are many such parallel relationships, the matching exercise is an efficient and effective testing procedure. A given number of premises, each of which constitutes a scoring unit, occupies much less space than would the comparable number of multiple-choice items. However, the matching exercise should be used only when every response is a plausible distracter for each of the premises. A useful rule is that the matching exercise should be used only when a number of possible multiple-choice stems require repetition of the same alternatives. Application of this rule helps to ensure that the matching form will be used only where it is naturally effective. When a teacher begins to construct a matching exercise, he frequently has two or three important relationships in mind and then seeks other relationships in order to complete the test. This artificial manufacture of matching items results in testing pupils' knowledge of some insignificant facts along with the original important ones, thus reducing the validity of the test.

The matching exercise can be scored on a completely objective basis. If each exercise is properly constructed with four or more responses, there is only a slight probability that the examinee can guess the correct answer. When used correctly, it has most of the advantages of the multiple-choice test and can be used to measure most of the same types of abilities.

Constructing the Matching Question. Many of the suggestions for the construction of other types of objective items apply to the writing of matching exercises. However, the following specific suggestions should also be helpful.

1. Make each matching exercise *homogeneous* in the sense that all premises and all responses refer to the same type of thing. The example on page 44 is homogeneous in that all the premises describe men active during the formation of the United States government, and all the responses are names of men prominent at that time. The following is a simple example of an exercise that is not homogeneous.

_____ 1. Largest city in Pennsylvania	a. William Penn
_____ 2. Flows through Harrisburg	b. Pittsburgh
_____ 3. Major steel-producing center	c. William Pitt
_____ 4. City located on one of the Great Lakes	d. Susquehanna River
	e. Philadelphia
_____ 5. Founder of Pennsylvania	f. Erie

Here we have three descriptions of cities, one of a river, and one of a man. The student who has no knowledge of Pennsylvania can easily get item 2 correct because only one river is listed among the responses. For item 5, he needs only to guess between the two men's names. In other words, the test's validity is greatly reduced because not all the responses are plausible distracters for all the premises.

2. Give a full and careful explanation of the basis for matching. If this is not done, some students may find a logical basis for matching different from the one intended. Below is an example of a poor exercise that could cause confusion.

_____	1. reclusive	a. ostracized
_____	2. gregarious	b. hermitic
_____	3. banished	c. social
		d. welcomed

A student without sufficient instructions might correctly match synonyms or antonyms. The necessary directions could say: "Choose from the righthand column the word that most closely defines each word in the lefthand column."

3. Make certain that all responses are plausible distracters for each premise. An important step in achieving this is to have homogeneous premises and responses, as described in suggestion 1 above. However, each exercise should also be checked to ensure that the examinee is not given unintended help by mixed plural and singular responses, by some premises beginning with *an* and others with *a,* or by other similar grammatical clues.

4. Limit the number of responses in a given matching exercise to about ten. Longer lists cause the examinee to waste time searching through the responses. If the original version of an exercise is too long, it should be divided into two or more separate exercises.

5. Avoid the "perfect matching" situation in which the number of premises is equal to the number of responses and each response is used only once. If the examinee knows all the associations except one, he will automatically get this final one correct also, thus diminishing the discriminating ability and the accuracy of the test as a measuring device.

6. Make sure that the list of premises contains the longer phrases or statements while the responses consist of short phrases, words, or symbols. This arrangement provides for more efficient use of pupil time in that the good student working any matching exercise will need to read each premise only once but will scan the list of responses several times (at least once with each premise).

7. Try to arrange the responses in some meaningful order. Arranging them alphabetically, chronologically, or on some logical basis should save the pupil time in finding the desired response.

8. The premises should be identified by number (since each one is a test item), and the responses should be identified by letter.

ASSEMBLING THE ITEMS INTO THE COMPLETED TEST FORM

The key step in the development of an achievement test is the actual writing of test items, but the writing of clear instructions and the planning of the format of the total test is also of major importance. If a test is to be effective, considerable attention must be given to its form. The examinee must understand what he is expected to do and should not be penalized because of poorly worded instructions, an inadequate scoring procedure, or other deficiencies in the mechanics of the test. Some suggestions that should be helpful in compiling test items to create the completed test form are listed below.

1. Give the student clear and complete instructions on how to answer items and record answers. If students miss items because they misunderstand the instructions, the test will yield invalid results. The instructions might well include a sample item and, if necessary, some practice exercises. To obtain ideas as to the best way to word instructions, the teacher should study the directions found with good published tests.

2. Group items of the same type together. Putting multiple-choice, true-false, and completion items together in one section of a test causes unnecessary confusion for the examinee. A set of instructions applicable to multiple-choice items should introduce a section of multiple-choice items. If another item type is to be used in the same test, these items also should be introduced with appropriate instructions.

3. Arrange the items in order of difficulty with the easier items near the beginning of the test. This arrangement will help to prevent a student from becoming stalled on a difficult item near the beginning of a test and therefore not having time to attempt later, easier items to which he knows the answers.

4. Fit the procedure for recording answers to the age level of the examinees. With older students, it is possible to employ a separate answer sheet and thereby simplify scoring without confusing students as to the mechanics of marking their answers. It is usually better to have very young students record their answers directly on the test sheet by circling the correct answer or drawing a line between two elements that are to be matched.

SUMMARY

Because teacher-made tests are undoubtedly the most widely used device for pupil evaluation, every teacher should be proficient in constructing them. The major types of item used are essay, supply, and selection (true-false, multiple-choice, and matching) items. Each type has certain strong as well as weak qualities and evaluates certain abilities more effectively than others. This chapter has enumerated these and has provided specific suggestions for writing the various types of item. The teacher who gives serious consideration to these suggestions should be able to improve the quality of his achievement tests.

Suggestions for Class Discussion and Further Investigation

1. Consider the following essay item: "Discuss the problem of defining educational objectives." How could this item be improved? Write a better version and then outline the ideal answer to it. Does outlining the answer lead you to see the need for possible changes in the wording of your item?
2. Examine the "test" below as a brief quiz covering the first three chapters of this text. Then list as many violations of valid test construction and item-writing as you can find.

TEST

1. _____ _____ should always be _____ in terms of _____ behavior.
2. The first major category in the *Taxonomy of Educational Objectives* by Blommers and others is knowledge.
3. The objective "The pupil will be able to use the rules for carrying to solve three-column addition problems" would be categorized under the taxonomy (a) category of knowledge, (b) category of translation, (c) category of application, (d) category of understanding, (e) category of appreciation.
4. Matching:

(a) true-false	(1) An author of *Taxonomy*
(b) multiple-choice	(2) Requires homogeneity of premises
(c) matching	
(d) S = R − W	(3) Best item type for measuring discriminating ability
(e) Bloom	(4) Correction for guessing formula
	(5) Tester has 50 percent chance of guessing answer

Suggestions for Further Reading

Since its publication, E. F. Lindquist's *Educational Measurement* (Washington, D.C.: American Council on Education, 1951) has come to be considered by many as providing the classic treatment of most topics relevant to the problem of constructing achievement tests; every student of educational testing should become familiar with it. Chapter 7, "Writing the Test Item," by Robert L. Ebel, and chapter 13, "The Essay Type of Examination," by John M. Stalnaker, will be particularly useful as supplementary readings on the topics of the construction of tests.

Many other sources discuss basic principles of item writing and deal with the problems of developing tests for various levels and subject-matter areas. The student will find the following sources valuable. Robert L. Ebel, *Measuring Educational Achievement* (Englewood Cliffs, N.J.: Prentice-Hall, 1965), chs. 4–6; Norman E. Gronlund, *Measurement and Evaluation in Teaching* (New York: Macmillan, 1965), chs. 7–10; C. M. Lindvall, *Testing and Evaluation: An Introduction* (New York: Harcourt, Brace & World, 1961), chs. 5–8; Julian C. Stanley, *Measurement in Today's Schools*, 4th ed. (Englewood Cliffs, N.J.: Prentice-Hall, 1964), chs. 7–8.

Chapter Four

Using Tests to Measure
Varied Types of Ability

Chapter three presented some basic principles of test construction and offered a variety of suggestions for writing specific types of test item. Following such suggestions should greatly improve the typical teacher's classroom tests. Although such improvement is highly desirable, even skillfully constructed tests make no real contribution to the improvement of evaluation and instruction if they measure limited and relatively unimportant learning. For example, an examination of a large sample of typical teacher-made tests would probably verify the charge that, for the most part, tests are limited to measuring knowledge of facts. Improving the technical quality of the items on such tests could greatly enhance their reliability and validity, but their scope should be enlarged so that they provide effective measures of additional and more complex pupil abilities.

OBJECTIVE-TYPE TESTS

Objective-type tests can be used to evaluate a variety of abilities. Many of the better published achievement tests contain items that require the examinee to interpret data, use generalizations to explain or predict results, apply procedures in order to arrive at answers, and demonstrate similar complex abilities. Also, many skilled teachers develop tests that measure some rather complex types of learning. This chapter will explain how objective-type test items can be used to measure several of the types of ability discussed in the *Taxonomy of Educational Objectives, Handbook I:*

Cognitive Domain[1] and will provide examples of items that measure each of those abilities.

Testing for Knowledge. Although too many tests can be justifiably criticized for consisting largely, or perhaps even solely, of items that measure only a pupil's knowledge or his ability to memorize, this does not mean that tests should contain no items measuring knowledge. The ultimate goal in most areas of study is the development of more complex abilities, but mastery of these abilities depends on the pupil's knowledge of certain principles, rules, procedures, and specific facts. Therefore, any comprehensive and diagnostic evaluation of a pupil's strengths and weaknesses in a given area must devote some attention to the knowledge that he possesses.

An important type of achievement in most subjects is knowledge of specifics—of persons, places, terminology, dates, sources, and similar data. The development of test items to measure knowledge of specifics is a rather straightforward task. A simple and effective procedure is to ask a specific question, as in the items shown in Figure 1. Although these items are in the multiple-choice form, it is obvious that with minor modifications these same questions could be transformed into supply-type items.

Figure 2 gives an example of how the incomplete statement form can be used to measure knowledge of specifics.

Although the multiple-choice and supply-type items are the forms that are most widely used for measuring knowledge, the matching exercise can be used effectively in many situations. One example of this is shown in Figure 3.

The beginning writer of objective-type test items is prone to rely rather exclusively on items that demand only a one- or two-word response, whether the items are multiple-choice, matching, or completion. This is a satisfactory and desirable practice as long as he is concerned only with measuring knowledge of specifics. However, most tests should also include some items evaluating the examinee's knowledge of principles, procedures, laws, and similar generalizations. The most effective objective-type item for this purpose is the multiple-choice item. Figure 4 shows examples of items using an incomplete statement as the stem and various phrases which complete the statement as responses. In items measuring knowledge of

---

1. Benjamin S. Bloom, ed. (New York: Longmans, Green and Co., 1956).

FIGURE 1

---

24. Which of the following men was a naturalist, noted for his study cf birds?
[e] Thoreau   [f] Mendel
[g] Burbank   [h] Audubon

---

68 Which permanent branch of the United Nations has direct control over specialized bodies such as the World Health Organization?
[e] Economic and Social Council
[f] Security Council
[g] International Court of Justice
[h] Trusteeship Council
[DK]

---

44. Which would you use to find whether Iowa is farther north than England?
1) A globe
2) A dictionary
3) An encyclopedia
4) A map of the United States

45. Where would you look for pictures of how people live in far-away countries?
1) In the *World Almanac*
2) In the *Reader's Digest*
3) In the *National Geographic Magazine*
4) In an atlas

Item 24 from Metropolitan Achievement Tests, High School Battery, Form Am, Test 11, Science Information. Reproduced by permission. Copyright 1962 by Harcourt, Brace & World, Inc., New York.

Item 68 from Cummings World History Test, Revised Edition, Form F. Reproduced by permission. Copyright © 1966. Copyright 1950 by Harcourt, Brace & World, Inc., New York.

Items 44 and 45 from Iowa Tests of Basic Skills, Multi-Level Edition for Grades 3–9, Form 1, Test W–3, Knowledge and Use of Reference Materials, Grade 6. Reproduced by permission. Copyright 1955 by the State University of Iowa, Houghton Mifflin Co., Boston.

FIGURE 2

---

23. All living things in contrast to nonliving things
    have —
    [a] brains   [b] organs
    [c] protoplasm   [d] tissues

Metropolitan Achievement Tests, High School Battery, Form
Am, Test 11, Science Information. Reproduced by permission.
Copyright 1962 by Harcourt, Brace & World, Inc., New York.

generalizations, it is necessary that the responses consist of something more than one or two words. Since this is the case, the use of
completion-type items would lead to considerable subjectivity in
scoring and a consequent reduction in reliability and validity. The
many difficulties involved in attempting to use a matching exercise
for measuring knowledge of generalizations should be obvious.

Figure 5 gives an example of another useful multiple-choice form
for evaluating an examinee's knowledge of various types of generalizations.

Testing for Comprehension. The second major category in the
taxonomy is comprehension. The abilities involved in this category
are frequently considered as aspects of "understanding." In helping
teachers to develop tests that measure a variety of abilities, the
writer has found it useful to give some attention to two subcategories of comprehension—*translation* and *interpretation.*

Translation is the ability to express a communication in words
or symbols different from those given. This may mean putting
something "in your own words," changing an expression from
mathematical symbols to verbal symbols or vice versa, or giving an

FIGURE 3

---

7. The author of *The Wealth of Nations.*   a. Hitler
                                                 b. John Locke
8. The author of *Mein Kampf.*   c. Marx
                                                 d. Rousseau
9. The author of *Capital.*   e. Adam Smith

Cummings World History Test, Form Am, Part A. Reproduced by permission.
Copyright 1950 by Harcourt, Brace & World, Inc., New York.

FIGURE 4

---

38. Transformers are used in electric power plants to —
    [e] change water power to electrical power
    [f] transform alternating current to direct current
    [g] transform direct current to alternating current
    [h] raise or lower the voltage in a power line

15. When there is a tie vote for the Presidency in the electoral college, the —
    [a] electoral college takes another vote
    [b] House of Representatives decides the election
    [c] people return to the polls to vote again
    [d] two political parties nominate new candidates

---

39 "Militarism" is a national policy which —

[a] opposes large standing armies and military preparedness

[b] glorifies great military deeds of the past rather than aggressive acts of the present

[c] emphasizes the need for secret police to maintain internal order

[d] supports powerful military forces dominated by an aggressive officer class

[DK]

Item 38 from Metropolitan Achievement Tests, High School Battery, Form Am, Test 11, Science Information, and item 15 from Metropolitan Achievement Tests, High School Battery, Form Am, Test 7, Social Studies. Reproduced by permission. Copyright 1962 by Harcourt, Brace & World, Inc., New York.

Item 39 from Cummings World History Test, Revised Edition, Form E. Reproduced by permission. Copyright © 1966. Copyright 1950 by Harcourt, Brace & World, Inc., New York.

example or an illustration. Although translation represents a minimum level of understanding, it is an essential ability in almost any area of study.

The ability to translate is measured by presenting the examinee with some type of communication and asking him either to con-

FIGURE 5

---

11 Interest is found by using the formula —

		a b c d
a lwh	c prt	
b prh	d hrw	11 ○ ○ ○ ○

---

23. Which of these is the most important characteristic of the *wise* consumer?

    a. He knows that the least expensive goods are the best buys.

    b. He knows that he must plan his spending.

    c. He knows that newspaper and radio advertising is generally false and misleading.

    d. He knows that the most expensive goods are highest in quality.

Item 11 from Stanford Achievement Test, Advanced Battery, Form X, Test 5, Arithmetic Concepts. Reproduced by permission. Copyright 1963, 1964 by Harcourt, Brace & World, Inc., New York.

Item 23 from Peltier-Durost Civics and Citizenship Test, Form Am, Part I. Reproduced by permission. Copyright 1958 by Harcourt, Brace & World, Inc., New York.

---

struct a translation of it or to identify the correct translation from several given choices. One method is shown in Figure 6, an item commonly found on reading comprehension tests. Note that each item asks a question for which the answer is a paraphrase of information presented in a sentence of the paragraph. As will be pointed out in our discussion of items that measure the ability to interpret, many reading-comprehension test items are somewhat more complex than this, requiring the combination of ideas from several sentences. Translation items, however, merely ask for a simple rephrasing of a communication without reorganization or summarization.

Items of this type can be used not only in evaluating general reading ability, but also in assessing the ability to translate material in such specific subject-matter areas as the sciences, the social studies, and foreign languages.

Figure 7 presents an example of another type of translation in which the pupil must be able to make the translation from a pictorial representation to the proper mathematical symbols.

FIGURE 6

While George Washington was president, the first United States mint was started at Philadelphia. Today the United States has a mint in Philadelphia, one in Denver, and one in San Francisco. All of our coins are made in these mints. You can tell where a coin was made by looking for the mint mark. The mint mark is a small letter. It is usually on the back of a coin. If a coin has a "D" on the back, it was made at the Denver mint. If it has an "S," it was made in San Francisco. If it has a "P," or if it has no mint mark at all, it was made in Philadelphia.

---

18. Where was the first United States mint?
1) In Washington   3) In Philadelphia
2) In Denver   4) In San Francisco

19. How many mints do we have now?
1) One   3) Three
2) Two   4) Four

20. What does the mint mark tell?
1) How old the coin is
2) Where the coin was made
3) How much the coin is worth
4) Who was president when the coin was made

21. If you want to see whether a coin has a mint mark, what will you look for?
1) A letter   3) A secret sign
2) A number   4) A man's name

FIGURE 7

66. Which of these addition examples is represented by the shaded parts of the diagrams below?

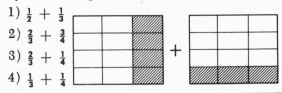

1) $\frac{1}{2} + \frac{1}{3}$
2) $\frac{2}{3} + \frac{3}{4}$
3) $\frac{2}{3} + \frac{1}{4}$
4) $\frac{1}{3} + \frac{1}{4}$

Additional examples of translation items useful in mathematics are shown in Figure 8. For item 17 the pupil must translate numerical data that tell him that a triangle has two equal sides into the equivalent description, "an isosceles triangle." In item 35 he must translate the pictorial representation of "the side opposite over the side adjacent" into its descriptive title "tangent of angle F." It should be noted that the pupil's ability to answer translation-type items always depends on his having certain knowledge. In items 17 and 35 he must know the definitions both of an isosceles triangle and of the tangent of an angle. However, the items require that he be able to translate these definitions into forms that are different from the original verbal statements. Translation builds on simple knowledge but involves an ability of a slightly more complex order. The categories of the taxonomy are arranged in a hierarchical order such that any of the higher-order abilities assume and build upon a pupil's command of the abilities that precede it in the taxonomy scale.

As suggested previously, *interpretation* refers to a slightly more complex form of comprehension than that involved in translation. It includes making some comparison among or summary of separate elements of a communication. The test items in Figure 9 may be used to illustrate the slight difference between translation and interpretation. Here the examinee is expected to answer certain questions concerning the tabular data. Item 33 would be considered a translation exercise. It involves the ability to recognize one item

FIGURE 8

---

17. Triangle *ABC* has sides $a = 12$ in., $b = 14$ in., and $c = 12$ in. *ABC* is an example of —

[a] an equilateral triangle
[b] a right triangle
[c] a scalene triangle
[d] an isosceles triangle

35. In the right triangle *EFG*, of which *FG* is the hypotenuse, the fraction f/g is designated as —

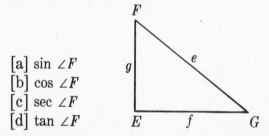

[a] sin ∠*F*
[b] cos ∠*F*
[c] sec ∠*F*
[d] tan ∠*F*

Metropolitan Achievement Tests, High School Battery, Form Am, Test 8, Mathematical Computation and Concepts. Reproduced by permission. Copyright 1962 by Harcourt, Brace & World, Inc., New York.

from the table when it is expressed in the form of a sentence (or, more correctly, a question and an answer). On the other hand, item 34 measures the ability to interpret. Here the examinee must read (translate) several items from the table and compare them; this is slightly more complex than simple translation. Similarly, the remaining items shown in Figure 9 also require comparisons among several items and hence should be considered as measuring the ability to interpret.

Figure 10 gives an example of an item that measures the examinee's ability to interpret verbal material. Interpretation receives major emphasis in many social studies courses, and hence items to measure it should be an important part of tests in these subjects. Another item that might be used in a social studies test is shown in Figure 11.

FIGURE 9

Monthly Average Temperature and Rainfall* in Selected
North American Cities
(Temperature in degrees; rainfall in inches)

	Fairbanks, Alaska		Memphis, Tenn.		Miami, Fla.		Phoenix, Ariz.		San Francisco, California	
	T	R	T	R	T	R	T	R	T	R
Jan.	—11	0.9	42	5.0	68	2.6	52	0.8	50	4.7
Feb.	0	0.5	44	4.2	68	2.0	56	0.8	53	3.8
Mar.	9	0.7	53	5.2	71	2.6	61	0.7	54	3.1
Apr.	29	0.3	62	4.9	74	3.4	68	0.4	56	1.5
May	47	0.7	70	4.0	77	6.5	76	0.1	57	0.7
June	58	1.4	78	3.6	80	7.1	85	0.1	59	0.2
July	60	1.8	81	3.1	82	6.0	90	1.0	59	0.0
Aug.	55	2.2	80	3.1	82	6.2	89	1.0	59	0.0
Sept.	44	1.3	74	2.8	81	9.0	83	0.9	62	0.3
Oct.	27	0.9	63	2.9	78	8.7	71	0.4	61	1.0
Nov.	3	0.7	52	4.2	72	2.8	60	0.7	57	2.5
Dec.	—8	0.6	44	4.5	69	1.9	53	0.9	52	4.4

*Includes snow, hail, sleet, etc.

33. **What is the average monthly rainfall for September
in Miami?**
   1) 1.3 inches   3) 9.0 inches
   2) 2.6 inches   4) 81 inches

34. **In which of these cities is April the driest month of
the year?**
   1) Fairbanks   3) Miami
   2) Memphis   4) San Francisco

35. **Which two cities have most nearly the same average
temperature in May?**
   1) Fairbanks and Memphis   3) Memphis and Miami
   2) Phoenix and San Francisco   4) Miami and Phoenix

36. **Which day generally is warmer, January 15 in Miami
or July 15 in San Francisco?**
   1) January 15 in Miami
   2) July 15 in San Francisco
   3) They are about equally warm.
   4) The table gives no clue to the answer.

37. **Which city may be said to have cool summers and
mild winters?**
   1) Fairbanks   3) Phoenix
   2) Memphis   4) San Francisco

FIGURE 10

---

24. "In three wealthy Northern states the average salary of teachers is three times that in the three poorest Southern states of the United States. However, the three poorest states have a higher tax in proportion to their income than do the wealthy states." For which of the following propositions is this statement the best evidence?

    f. State governments should increase their contributions to local school districts.
    g. The South is not interested in good education.
    h. Education should be controlled by the national government.
    i. Federal financial aid to education is necessary.
    j. Some teachers are paid more than they are worth.

Dimond-Pflieger Problems of Democracy Test, Form Am, Part A. Reproduced by permission. Copyright 1953 by Harcourt, Brace & World, Inc., New York.

Since the ability to interpret written material is essential in all subject-matter areas, it would seem important to test for this ability in connection with most subjects. An example of how this may be done is shown in Figure 12. Although these items deal with science data, it should be obvious that this same procedure can be used with almost any subject. The essential step is to present the examinee with some reading material new to him (so that he cannot answer the items from previously acquired knowledge) and then prepare items that the pupil can answer only if he relates ideas from several different parts of the communication. An efficient procedure, one that is followed with most reading-comprehension tests, is to base some translation and some interpretation items on the same reading passage.

Testing for Application. Most teachers probably like to feel that pupils in their classes are learning to apply what they know. If application is a real goal in any particular instructional situation, then the tests that are used to evaluate achievement must include items that measure the pupil's ability to make applications.

The taxonomy suggests that application means

the use of abstractions in particular and concrete situations. The abstractions may be in the form of general ideas, rules of procedures, or generalized methods. The abstractions may also be technical principles, ideas, and theories which must be remembered and applied.[2]

This makes it clear that what is applied in any situation is not facts or data but rules or principles that describe the relationships between facts or that spell out methods or procedures. The first task of the teacher, then, in developing test materials to measure the ability "to apply" is to identify exactly what the pupil is expected to be able to apply. The teacher should ask himself: "What are the principles, rules, or procedures that have been studied in this unit?" The second and related step is to determine exactly what is involved in the application of a given rule or generalization. Among the possible results of an application are the following. A pupil may apply a principle or a procedure to:

1. produce an outcome.
2. develop a plan for producing a desired result.
3. explain some reported or existing outcome.
4. predict a consequence.

Some procedures for evaluating these various types of application are suggested in the following sections.

1. Application to produce an outcome This ability is involved in such tasks as applying certain principles and procedures to arrive at an answer to a "story problem" in arithmetic, using rules of punctuation and capitalization to produce a correctly written paragraph, or applying certain principles to produce a desired result in a science laboratory demonstration. The evaluation of abilities of this type frequently can best be done through nontesting procedures or by using an essay examination. However, objective-type items can also be of some use. Figure 13 shows examples of how objective-type items can test the pupil's ability to apply procedures to produce results in mathematics.

Figure 14 illustrates a way in which a student's ability to apply rules of punctuation and capitalization can be tested objectively.

2. Application to plan for a desired outcome The application of certain principles or procedures involves tasks of such magnitude and complexity that it is unrealistic to have the pupil actually carry them out. However, in such cases it may be meaningful to ask the student to explain what should be done to achieve a desired

---

2. *Ibid.,* p. 205.

Use the poster below to answer questions 88–92

RE-ELECT
JOHN DOE

① HAS SPENT FIVE TERMS IN HOUSE OF REPRESENTATIVES.
② BELIEVES GOVERNMENT SPENDING MUST DECREASE.
③ AGAINST CREEPING SOCIALISM.
④ FAVORS REDUCTION OF FARM SUBSIDIES.
⑤ CHAMPION OF FREE ENTERPRISE.
⑥ SUPPORTS INCREASED FOREIGN AID.
⑦ MEMBER HOUSE FOREIGN RELATIONS COMMITTEE.

U. S. HOUSE OF REPRESENTATIVES

88 Which two items on the poster indicate Mr. Doe's success as a politician?

5 ① and ②   7 ① and ⑦
6 ② and ③   8 ③ and ⑤

88 ○ 5 ○ 6 ○ 7 ○ 8

89 Which item most clearly indicates that Mr. Doe, if elected, would not support socialized medicine?

1 ③   3 ⑤
2 ②   4 ⑥

89 ○ 1 ○ 2 ○ 3 ○ 4

90 Which two items on the poster appear to be inconsistent?

5 ② and ③   7 ④ and ⑤
6 ③ and ④   8 ② and ⑥

90 ○ 5 ○ 6 ○ 7 ○ 8

91 Which items on the poster most specifically indicate Mr. Doe's political philosophy?

1 ②, ③, and ⑤
2 ③, ④, and ⑤
3 ①, ③, and ⑤
4 ②, ④, and ⑤

91 ○ 1 ○ 2 ○ 3 ○ 4

92 For how many years has Mr. Doe served in the Congress?

5 five   7 ten
6 fifteen   8 thirty

92 ○ 5 ○ 6 ○ 7 ○ 8

outcome, in which case he may devise a plan of action. A modified approach to the evaluation of this ability is to use objective-type test items in which the examinee is asked to identify the essential element or essential step in a plan for attaining a desired goal. Examples of such items are shown in Figure 15. Note that the stem of the item describes a situation and the desired result. The examinee identifies from the responses the proper procedure to apply. The items require that the pupil know certain principles and that he apply them to tell what should be done to achieve a specified outcome.

Another example of an item designed to measure a pupil's ability to develop a plan that will produce a desired result is shown in Figure 16. Here the item could have required the student to produce the result—that is, calculate the length of the specified line— but the item is instead concerned with whether the pupil can identify the procedure that should be used to obtain the result.

3. Application to explain an outcome   The ability to tell why some given situation exists by applying the pertinent principle can be measured directly through the use of multiple-choice items. The general procedure is to describe a particular situation and the expected outcome and then ask the examinee to choose the principle that best explains it. Figure 17 provides several examples of items of this type.

4. Application to predict an outcome   Another important way in which principles may be applied is in predicting an outcome— particularly in the physical and social sciences. Figure 18 presents an item measuring this ability in a social science area. Here the pupil has to apply what he has learned about the law and the operation of the courts in order to tell what will happen in a specific situation.

Examples of multiple-choice items to measure this prediction ability in general science are shown in Figure 19. Note that in each of these items some situations with respect to natural phenomena are described, and the examinee is expected to predict what will result from the given conditions.

FIGURE 11

FIGURE 12

Questions 27-30 relate to the following information:

The Earth's crust conceals many activities that are mysteries to man.

Every so often evidences of these activities, such as earthquakes and volcanoes, appear. These are probably the most spectacular evidences of the tremendous heat and pressures that exist below the Earth's crust.

In September, 1957, a new volcano arose from the sea near Fayal in the Azores. Lava burst forth with such force that some gases and steam and glowing lava ascended a half mile into the atmosphere. A new island was formed by this volcano. A month later the entire volcano disappeared beneath the ocean. A week later, it reappeared closer to the mainland, still belching lava bombs and gases. Several minor eruptions followed, and each time more land arose from the sea. The final result was the creation of a new peninsula. The main volcano, called Ilha Nova, is still erupting. Eventually its activity will cease, and the forces of nature, such as erosion, may make the new peninsula a habitable land.

27 The eruption of Ilha Nova was apparently the result of

    A   changes on the Earth's surface.

    B   heat and pressure below the Earth's surface.

    C   uneven movements of the ocean.

    D   forces of erosion.

    E   an earthquake.

29 The creation of a new peninsula as a result of volcanic activity suggests that

    A   there are no volcanic eruptions in the ocean.

    B   the oceans are diminishing in size.

    C   volcanoes are active for only brief periods of time.

    D   the adjacent land may have been formed in the same way.

    E   the adjacent land may sink eventually into the ocean.

FIGURE 13

POTATO SALAD

2 tablespoons vinegar
$5\frac{1}{2}$ cups sliced, cooked potatoes
$1\frac{2}{3}$ cups sliced cucumbers
$\frac{3}{4}$ cup chopped green pepper
$1\frac{1}{2}$ cups chopped celery
1 12-ounce can luncheon meat, cubed
1 cup salad dressing
$1\frac{1}{4}$ teaspoons salt

Serves 8

---

75. Mrs. Alden used the recipe above to make salad for 12. How many cups of sliced, cooked potatoes did she need?

    1) $2\frac{3}{4}$　　2) **7**　　3) $8\frac{1}{4}$　　4) (Not given)

94. In a recent year, the winner of the state high school basketball tournament won 23 of the 26 games played during the season. To the nearest tenth, what per cent of its games did the team win?

    1) **88.5**　　　　　　3) **87.0**
    2) **88.4**　　　　　　4) (Not given)

95. The starting five for the championship team had heights of 6 ft. 2 in., 6 ft. 1 in., 6 ft. 8 in., 5 ft. 11 in., and 6 ft. What was the team's average height?

    1) **6 ft.**　　　　　　3) **6 ft. 2 in.**
    2) **6 ft. 1 in.**　　　　4) (Not given)

96. The total attendance for the 8 sessions of the state tournament was 81,251. The previous year the total attendance was 73,986. To the nearest whole per cent, what was the per cent of increase in attendance?

    1) **10**　　　　　　　3) **8**
    2) **9**　　　　　　　4) (Not given)

Part C
Punctuation and Capitalization
DIRECTIONS

A number of punctuation marks and capital letters are needed in the sentences below. Read each sentence through. Then look at each place to which an arrow points (to a *letter* or a *space*) and decide what change is needed there, if any. Find the row of answer spaces at the right which has the same number as the arrow and put a cross through your answer. NP stands for *No Punctuation* needed. If you do not know the answer, mark DK (for don't know). Study the samples below. They have been marked correctly.

A	[O]	[⊠]	[NP]	[DK]
B	[⊠]	[,]		[DK]

SAMPLES Lindbergh flew alone across the atlantic ocean
(A)→ (B)→

The manager of the hotel carleton said i could keep trixy in the basement
(46)→ (47)→ (48)→

46	[h]	[H]		[DK]
47	[i]	[I]		[DK]
48	[t]	[T]		[DK]

Jack doyle who was my fathers closest friend has moved to utica new york
(49)→ (50)→ (51)→ (52)→

49	[,]	[.]	[NP]	[DK]
50	[;]		[NP]	[DK]
51	[,]	["]	[NP]	[DK]
52	[:]	[,]	[NP]	[DK]

We shall meet our cousin in front of the drug store on elm street
(53)→ (54)→ (55)→

53	[c]	[C]		[DK]
54	[s]	[S]		[DK]
55	[e]	[E]		[DK]

Theyve always attended services at the west baptist church on thanksgiving
(56)→ (57)→ (58)→ (59)→ (60)→

56	[']	[NP]		[DK]
57	[w]	[W]		[DK]
58	[b]	[B]		[DK]
59	[c]	[C]		[DK]
60	[t]	[T]		[DK]

Either you will go with me or you will not go at all his father shouted
(61)→ (62)→ (63)→

61	["]	[NP]		[DK]
62	[;]	[!]	[NP]	[DK]
63	[;]	[,]	[NP]	[DK]

Evaluating Other Abilities. It has been found that objective-type test items can be used quite successfully to measure the abilities of knowledge, translation, interpretation, and application discussed in preceding sections. Work carried out by the writer and his students indicates that most items on published achievement tests can be categorized as measuring one of these abilities, leading to the suggestion that, if the beginning teacher will learn to develop such items, he will be in a position to produce tests that are about as comprehensive in types of abilities sampled as objective-type tests can be. This would probably mean that his tests could be more comprehensive than those of the average teacher. However, if he relies solely on objective-type tests for assessing the achievement of his pupils, he will still fail to evaluate certain important abilities. To assess abilities that are beyond the level of "application" in the hierarchical order of the taxonomy categories, procedures other than objective-type testing will have to be employed, despite the fact that the taxonomy gives examples of objective-type items that can be used to measure analysis, synthesis, and evaluation. Persons sophisticated in test-development procedures may be able to develop items for this purpose, but the less skilled person will usually end up with items that are actually measuring some simpler ability such as comprehension or application.

Synthesis is certainly an obvious and essential ability that all teachers will want to evaluate. In most subject-matter areas we are concerned with the pupil's ability to produce or create something—a sentence, a paragraph, or a longer composition—and the obvious means of such evaluation is an essay examination or an out-of-class assignment. In some subjects we may be concerned with the student's ability actually to synthesize or produce some physical object —a painting or other work of art, a poster, an industrial arts project, or something from the home economics kitchen. Here also the means of evaluation is rather obvious. We must first ask the pupil to create the product under certain conditions and then assess either the procedure he uses, the product itself, or both. With some evi-

---

FIGURE 14

Metropolitan Achievement Tests, Intermediate Battery, Form A, Test 4, Part C. Reproduced by permission. Copyright 1958 by Harcourt, Brace & World, Inc., New York.

FIGURE 15

---

17 In developing a new blueberry, which one of the following is most apt to produce a sweeter, larger berry?

[a] Cross-pollinate very sweet berries with very large berries.

[b] Self-pollinate very large berries.

[c] Self-pollinate very sweet berries.

[d] Plant the cuttings of very sweet berries near the cuttings of large berries.

[DK]

50 Two scientists, supported by a balloon filled with helium gas, ascend to a height of 20,000 feet. They have with them 2 extra tanks of compressed helium and 10 heavy canvas bags each filled with sand and fastened to a strong 100-foot rope. To stop the balloon and take some measurements at 10,000 feet, the scientists must —

[e] pour out one or more bags of sand

[f] lower one or more of the bags of sand to the full length of the rope

[g] release some of the helium from the balloon

[h] let some of the compressed gas from the tanks flow into the balloon

[DK]

Item 17 from Read General Science Test, Revised Edition, Form F, and item 50 from Read General Science Test, Revised Edition, Form E. Reproduced by permission. Copyright 1950, © 1965 by Harcourt, Brace & World, Inc., New York.

FIGURE 16

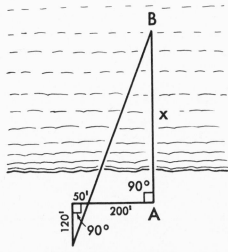

136. Some Boy Scouts determined indirectly the distance *x* from a point A in the city park to a buoy B in the river by making the measurements shown on the above drawing. Which one of these proportions could be used to find the distance *x*?

1) $\dfrac{x}{120} = \dfrac{200}{50}$ 3) $\dfrac{x}{200} = \dfrac{50}{120}$

2) $\dfrac{x}{50} = \dfrac{200}{120}$ 4) $\dfrac{x}{120} = \dfrac{50}{200}$

Iowa Tests of Basic Skills, Multi-Level Edition for Grades 3–9, Form 1, Test A–1, Arithmetic Concepts, Grades 8 and 9. Reproduced by permission. Copyright 1955 by the State University of Iowa, Houghton Mifflin Co., Boston.

FIGURE 17

---

10 For farming, plains usually produce more than hills
because —

    5 topsoil erodes more easily from
      hills than from plains
    6 there is more rainfall on the
      plains
    7 the plains are warmer   5 6 7 8
    8 winds harm crops on the hills 10 ○ ○ ○ ○

11 Southern Italy has a mild climate because it is —

    1 far south, like Egypt
    2 tempered by winds from the
      Mediterranean
    3 warmed by winds from North
      Africa
    4 protected on the north by high   1 2 3 4
      mountains   11 ○ ○ ○ ○

12 In the movement of people westward, it was more
difficult to use river boats west of the Mississippi
because the —

    5 rivers were deep
    6 Indians were more dangerous
    7 boats had to go upstream   5 6 7 8
    8 rivers flowed too slowly 12 ○ ○ ○ ○

---

    6. In earlier periods, Greek, Latin, and French
        have all been desirable second languages
        for educated people. Which best explains
        why English is now a more popular second
        language than any of those?
      6–1 English is closely associated with
           Christianity.
      6–2 English is now the first language for
           over half the people in the world.
      6–3 A large proportion of world trade
           is carried on by English-speaking
           people.
      6–4 English is more easily learned than
           any other modern language.
      6–5 All scientific works are published in
           English. . . . . .6(   )

Items 10, 11, and 12 from Stanford Achievement Test, Advanced Battery, Form X, Test 7, Social Studies, Part A, Content. Reproduced by permission. Copyright 1963, 1964 by
Harcourt, Brace & World, Inc., New York.

7 One gets out of breath more easily on a high
mountain trail than along a seashore because
on a high mountain

   A   gravity exerts greater pull.
   B   the circulation of blood is more rapid.
   C   the circulation of blood is slower.
   D   less oxygen enters the blood.
   E   a person's pulse beat is slower.

15 It is impossible to hear a bell ringing in a vacuum
because

   A   there is no material in the vacuum through
       which sound waves can travel.
   B   the vacuum acts as a sound conductor.
   C   the clapper gives up kinetic energy to the
       vacuum.
   D   the vacuum decreases the pitch of the bell.
   E   the vacuum increases the pitch of the bell.

Item 6 from Cooperative World History Test, Form Y, Part II.
Reproduced by permission. Copyright 1948, Cooperative Test
Division, Educational Testing Service, Princeton, New Jersey.

Items 7 and 15 from Cooperative Science Test, Form A, General
Science. Reproduced by permission. Copyright 1962, Coopera-
tive Test Division, Educational Testing Service, Princeton, New
Jersey.

FIGURE 18

34. The case of Sam Suspect has been tried, but
the jury cannot come to an agreement.
What will happen now?

   34–1   Sam will be compensated for the
          time lost from work.
   34–2   The case will be retried with a new
          jury.
   34–3   The judge will send the case to a
          higher court.
   34–4   The trial will begin all over, and the
          same jury will try again to reach a
          verdict.
   34–5   The judge will determine the ver-
          dict. . . . . 34(   )

Cooperative American Government Test, Form Y, Part I. Reproduced by permission. Copyright 1948, Cooperative Test Division,
Educational Testing Service, Princeton, New Jersey.

33 According to the chart below, which is the best weather prediction for Saturday?

	THURSDAY 6 A.M.	THURSDAY 6 P.M.	FRIDAY 6 A.M.	FRIDAY 6 P.M.
Barometer	30.00	30.01	29.98	30.00
Temperature	44°F.	36° F.	30°F.	20° F.
Wind Direction	West	North-west	North	North
Clouds	Cumulus	Cumulus	None	Cumulus
Weather	Rain	Clearing	Clear	Clear

[a] snow, clearing
[b] rain, colder
[c] clear, colder
[d] snow, colder
[DK]

9 Mars has two natural satellites, Phobos and Deimos. The orbit of Phobos is closer to Mars than is that of Deimos, and Phobos moves at a faster rate of speed than Deimos. Therefore, which of the following must be true?

A   Deimos makes more trips around Mars in a year than does Phobos.

B   Phobos makes more trips around Mars in a year than does Deimos.

C   Deimos is larger than Phobos.

D   Phobos is larger than Deimos.

E   Phobos will eventually strike Mars.

18 If you travel far north of your home, which of the following will be true?

F   The North Star will appear higher in the sky.

G   The Sun will always rise earlier.

H   You will pass through several time zones.

J   The stars will move toward the west faster than when you are at home.

K   The stars will move toward the east faster than when you are at home.

dence of an increasing emphasis on creativity as a goal of education, it would seem that the evaluation of a pupil's ability with respect to synthesis should receive increased attention.

Although we have thus far been concerned largely with cognitive abilities, the teacher must always be concerned with the central importance of such affective variables as interests and attitudes. In the first chapter we pointed out that because present devices for measuring variables in the affective domain are complex and relatively ineffective, little space would be devoted to them here. However, the teacher should be vitally concerned with the attitudes and interests of his students, even though he will probably have to assess them through informal, nonobjective procedures. But such procedures can be very useful. Certainly the interests of a student can be investigated by talking to him, by listening, and by observing his choices and other actions. Such information can be useful in judging the effectiveness of teaching procedures and materials and in planning pupil activities.

SUMMARY

A common and frequently justifiable complaint about classroom tests is that they measure only limited types of abilities, typically the knowledge of facts. However, tests can be used to measure a variety of abilities. This chapter has shown how objective-type test items can be used to measure such cognitive abilities as knowledge of specifics, knowledge of generalizations, translation, interpretation, and application. The teacher who plans his evaluation instruments with the proper care and who employs some of the procedures described here should be able to develop tests that effectively measure such proficiencies. The assessment of higher-level cognitive abilities such as synthesis will probably require the use of such nonobjective procedures as essay examinations, out-of-class assign-

---

FIGURE 19

ments, and the observation of pupil performance. The last of these procedures will also be used in appraising important affective variables such as attitudes and interests. Techniques for evaluating a great variety of instructional objectives are available to the teacher willing to take the time to learn how to use them and expend the effort needed in using them.

Suggestions for Class Discussion and Further Investigation

1. Develop an objective-type test for a subject-matter area that is of concern to you, making certain to include some items that measure each of the following abilities: knowledge of specifics, knowledge of generalization, translation, interpretation, application.
2. Figure 13 presents examples of test items measuring a type of application ability. Such items typically require that the examinee possess certain knowledge of specifics and of rules or principles as well as certain abilities in translation. For each item in Figure 13 identify the abilities needed to answer the item.
3. For a subject of concern to you identify some pupil ability that has a certain degree of complexity (such as that represented by the test items in Figure 13). Identify the subabilities (perhaps those involving knowledge, translation, etc.) essential to mastery of the complex task. How might you develop a diagnostic test to determine the pupil's strengths and weaknesses in those subabilities?
4. Secure a copy of at least one standardized achievement test battery. Categorize every item in each test in the battery according to the taxonomy category that you feel it measures (as you did in chapter two). Compare the various subject-matter areas in terms of percentage of items measuring the different taxonomy abilities. What are the implications of any differences among subjects for what is stressed in typical teaching or testing in each subject?

Suggestions for Further Reading

In concerning himself with ways of evaluating a variety of types of pupil abilities, the reader should study again the

Taxonomy of Educational Objectives, Benjamin S. Bloom, ed. (New York: Longmans, Green and Co., 1956), giving careful attention to sample test items and to the suggestion for testing in the various categories.

Further suggestions and examples will be found in: Edward J. Furst, *Constructing Evaluation Instruments* (New York: David McKay Co., 1958), chs. 8–10; J. Raymond Gerberich, *Specimen Objective Test Items* (New York: David McKay Co., 1956); C. M. Lindvall, *Testing and Evaluation: An Introduction* (New York: Harcourt, Brace & World, 1961), chs. 7–8.

Chapter Five

Using Statistics
to Derive Test Scores

As we indicated in chapter one, the concern of educators with procedures for evaluation and testing is basically a concern with the problem of how best to acquire necessary information about pupils. Such information is frequently gathered through rather informal procedures, and many records are based on verbal statements about pupil ability, aptitude, personality, and interest. However, for a variety of reasons it is generally desirable to supplement informal procedures with techniques that yield some type of quantitative data—with tests, inventories, and rating scales.

THE NEED FOR QUANTITATIVE MEASUREMENT

In most areas of human concern—in various sciences, disciplines, and technologies—increased understanding and mastery have been accompanied by increased skill in quantifying the variables. Progress in science and technology has been accompanied by the change from rather gross, general descriptions to relatively precise measurement of important characteristics and qualities. Cave men using a pole to pry or lift a rock probably knew that the difficulty of the task varied with the length of the pole and the location of the fulcrum. However, when this principle of the lever was applied to complex machinery, relationships of this type had to be expressed in quantitative terms. The reader can undoubtedly think of a great number of other examples where development in a given field has been related to success in obtaining precise measures of variables and in expressing relationships in quantitative terms. Although many of the human characteristics involved in learning and instruction may never be measurable, tests and other instruments for measuring some of the important variables have been devised. Tests for assessing achievement, aptitude, interests, and attitudes have made it possible for instructors to obtain more precise information about their students and have enabled researchers to make studies of the relationships among a variety of variables involved in human learning.

As is true of persons working in more basic scientific areas, teachers and others dealing with the problems of education realize certain benefits from advances in developing tests and other devices for obtaining quantitative descriptions of pertinent variables.

1. Quantification provides for more exact description The teacher who knows that three pupils have IQ's of 95, 115, and 142, as determined by the Stanford-Binet test, has more exact information about these pupils than he would have if they had been described to him as "average," "a little above average," and "very high" in their academic aptitudes.

2. Quantitative procedures are generally marked by greater objectivity The application of some test or instrument yielding a numerical measure typically is sufficiently independent of the person applying it that two persons would obtain essentially the same measure if they each applied the same instrument to the same subject. This probability of essential agreement in results makes the resulting data more reliable than are those obtained by more subjective procedures.

3. Quantitative procedures permit clearer and more efficient communication Whether the communication is a discussion between two teachers or is the transmittal of a pupil's records from one school district to another, the usefulness of the information is usually enhanced if it includes scores on certain standard tests. A rather extended written or oral communication would be required to convey anywhere near the same amount of information as that contained in a score on a test well known to both participants. Verbal descriptions, although frequently helpful, are not as economical or as precise as is quantitative information.

MEASUREMENT THEORY

Although the use of a variety of types of instrument helps teachers and administrators to realize benefits, educational and psychological tests do not derive the same type of measure as that resulting from the use, for example, of a tape measure to determine linear distances. The tape measure and most other devices for measuring physical qualities have two characteristics that enable them to yield relatively pure measures: (1) *an absolute zero point*—if anything should measure "zero" when the tape is applied, it would have "no length whatsoever"; and (2) *equal intervals*—equal differences between measures at any point along the scale indicate equal differences in length (the quality being measured).

These qualities of linear measuring devices seem rather simple and obvious, but they take on more meaning when we look for the same qualities in an educational or psychological test. In an achievement test, whether it is an essay examination or an objective-type test, the student is asked to respond to certain questions so that we can obtain a measure of his command of a certain subject. If he does not respond correctly to any question, he receives a score of zero. However, we cannot assume that this means he knows absolutely nothing about the subject being tested. His zero score was determined by the difficulty of the questions as well as by his command of the subject. He might have been able to answer correctly a few simpler questions about the subject and to receive some score above zero. His score on the original test is not an *absolute* zero in the sense of telling us that he has "no knowledge whatsoever" of the subject.

Also, as is probably obvious, the scale of scores produced by a test does not have equal intervals. Let us imagine a spelling test of fifty words ranging from quite simple to relatively difficult. The difference between a score of 25 and one of 20 may indicate the ability to spell five words of moderate difficulty. However, the difference between a score of 50 and one of 45 would probably indicate the ability to spell five very difficult words. In these two cases the differences in score are equal (5 points in each case) but do not represent equal differences in spelling ability. This same lack of knowledge about the absolute difficulty of the components of a test means that all educational and psychological tests produce scales that probably do not consist of equal units. A casual consideration of this problem might suggest that we could solve it by assigning weights to the various parts of an essay test or to each item in an objective-type test. Although in some cases this might correct some rather gross inequalities, the use of subjective judg-

ient in this way would be no guarantee that the measuring scale
ould be so refined as to yield equal intervals.

The difference between the absolute type of measurement result-
ig when a tape measure is used to determine linear distances and
ie type resulting when a psychological test is used to measure a
iental quality may become clear if we consider two possible ways
f measuring the heights of pupils.

In the first and more obvious method, each pupil stands with his
.ack to the wall, heels on the floor, and a tape measure is used to
letermine the distance from the floor to a point on the wall hori-
ontally even with the top of his head. The second procedure,
oughly paralleling our mental testing procedures, would have each
)upil stand next to a table; we would then measure his height
.bove the table by stacking a neat column of blocks on the table
intil the height of the stacked blocks reached the height of the
)upil's head. To make this second procedure equivalent to the
ieasuring procedure in educational and psychological testing, we
vould have to assume that it is impossible for us to determine the
ieight of the table and that the blocks used are of varying and
indetermined thickness. We would have a zero point, the top of
:he table—certainly not an absolute zero—and unequal units on the
.cale, the thickness of the blocks.

This illustration can be helpful to us as an analogy, not only in
thinking about the weaknesses in the measures obtained from
tests, but also in recognizing the value of these less-than-perfect
measures.

It would probably be agreed that if the table-and-blocks method
for measuring height were the only procedure available, it would
yield more useful information than mere verbal descriptions such
as "quite tall," "of average height," and "very short." Measures obtained in this way, despite their limitations, should at least be quite
useful in describing the relative heights of the pupils. In a similar
manner, educational and psychological tests, despite limitations in
the type of measure they produce, can be very useful in describing
the various mental qualities with which they are concerned. The
informed educator, recognizing that test scores do not represent a
perfect type of measurement, will not be tempted to give such
scores an unwarranted exact meaning, but at the same time will
use these less-than-perfect measures to serve the essential purposes
for which they are important and appropriate.

DERIVED SCORES

As has been suggested, limitations in exactness of measurement mean that scores from educational and psychological tests have little absolute meaning. They may tell us how many items a student has answered correctly or what proportion of the relevant material he has covered in his essay, but they do not give us an absolute measure such as we obtain when we use a tape measure to determine distance. For many purposes it would be highly desirable to have some means of obtaining "content referenced" scores—scores, comparable to measures of distance, with one number that would give us rather exact information as to where a person stands with respect to the mastery of a given body of content. This is of course not possible with current instruments and procedures in which two persons may earn the same score on a test, having answered different combinations of items to achieve that score. Such scores do not give us very exact information about the specific content pupils have mastered.

Because of the lack of success in developing "content referenced" scores, test users must rely largely on "norm referenced" scores that compare a given score with others in a norm group. Pupils who have just had their corrected test papers returned to them with the raw score shown at the top of each paper quickly attempt to determine the real meaning of a score by comparing it with their neighbors' scores. They seek answers to such questions as: "Where do I rank among all members of the class?" and "Where does my score stand with respect to the average for the class?" In much the same way, teachers and school administrators are frequently concerned with such questions as: "How do my pupils compare with pupils in other classes?" and "How does our school rank in comparison with other schools?" A raw score on a test takes on meaning only when it is compared with the scores of other persons who have taken the same test. For this reason a variety of procedures have been developed for transforming raw scores into types of scores that tell something about the relative meaning of a given performance.

The Letter-Grade as a Derived Score. Perhaps the most common procedure classroom teachers use to attach some relative meaning to raw scores made by pupils on teacher-made tests is to assign letter grades to the scores. Although different teachers use varying degrees of refinement in such grading, the general procedure is to assign "A" to some top percentage, "B" to some percentage of scores just below that, and so on. A teacher will vary the percentage of persons receiving a given grade from one test to another on the basis of the nature of the distribution of scores, on the basis of the absolute performance on the test, and on similar, rather subjective bases, but the transformation of a raw score to a letter grade does provide the pupil with a derived "score" that tells him something about how well he did in relation to other pupils. This is a useful procedure, but not nearly as exact or as meaningful as other types of transformation.

The Percentile Rank. The rather obvious and direct way of interpreting a raw score so that it tells something about an individual's performance in comparison with other persons in a given group is to report on his relative rank within the group. This would mean saying such things as "This is the highest score in the class," "This score ranked third from the top," or "This score ranked twenty-seventh from the top." The only difficulty with this procedure is that it does not take into account the size of the group. To overcome this difficulty the *percentile rank* (also called the "centile rank") is used. The percentile rank is a number that tells what percentage of individuals within the specified norm group scored lower than the raw score in question. That is, if the percentile rank corresponding to a raw score of 37 is 68, 68 percent of the individuals in the norm group had raw scores lower than 37.

A simple procedure for computing percentile ranks will illustrate their meaning and can also be used for the actual transformation of raw scores to percentile ranks. The following formula (where N is the total number of pupils) is applied:

[Eq. 1]

$$\text{percentile rank} = \frac{\text{number of persons below score} + \frac{1}{2} \text{ of persons at score}}{N} \times 100$$

Assume that the numbers shown below represent scores on a certain test for 30 pupils in a given class.

71	65	61	60	57	52
69	64	61	60	57	50
67	63	61	59	56	47
66	63	60	59	55	46
65	62	60	58	54	43

To determine the percentile rank of a score of 57, we would note that eight pupils have scores lower than this and that two pupils have scores at 57. Substituting 30 for N in Equation 1, we would have

$$\text{percentile rank} = \frac{8+1}{30} \times 100 = 30$$

That is, 30 is the percentile rank of a raw score of 57.

To determine the percentile rank of a raw score of 62, we note that 20 pupils have scores lower than 62 and that only one pupil has a score at 62. The percentile rank of 62 would then be

$$\text{percentile rank} = \frac{20+0.5}{30} \times 100 = 68.3$$

Note that when only one person has received the raw score for which the percentile rank is being determined, we add one half of one, or 0.5, to the number of persons below the score. This procedure emphasizes the fact that we are determining the percentile rank of a *point* on the score scale. Under the usual assumption concerning the value of a raw score on a test, the raw score of 62 occupies the interval of 61.5 to 62.5. The exact point 62 is then at the mid-point of this interval, and it is logical to assume that at a score of 62 (that is, from 61.5 to 62.5), half the persons score above and half score below the exact point of 62.

A further study of statistical methods will reveal a variety of formulas and procedures for determining percentile ranks, including graphic methods and methods for use with grouped frequency distributions. However, all these procedures are either equivalent to or approximations of the procedure presented here. Some of them may be simpler to use under certain circumstances, but the present method is always usable when raw scores are available.

In many circumstances, particularly in the use of standardized tests, the term percentile (or centile) is used in conjunction with tables of *percentile ranks*. It is important to grasp the distinction between these two terms. If the raw score of 57 has a percentile rank of 30, then the thirtieth percentile in this distribution is 57. That is, the *percentile rank* is a number that tells the *percent* of persons scoring below a particular point on the score scale. On the other hand, the *percentile* is a *point on the score scale* such that the indicated percent of persons falls below it.

STANDARD SCORES

Another procedure for giving relative meaning to a raw score on a test is to speak of it in terms of whether it is above or below "average" and how far above or below it is. A somewhat refined procedure for doing this is represented by the *standard score.* A standard score tells us how far any given performance is above or below the arithmetic *mean* in terms of the relative variability of the distribution as measured by the *standard deviation.* Understanding the standard score, then, requires some comprehension of the two statistics upon which it is based, the *mean* and the *standard deviation.*

The Arithmetic Mean. Most persons are well acquainted with the arithmetic mean, or merely the mean. It is what is commonly implied when we speak of the "average" of a set of numbers or measures. It is determined by dividing the sum of all the measures by the number of measures involved. This method is commonly represented by the formula

$$M = \frac{\Sigma X}{N} \qquad \text{[Eq. 2]}$$

where M represents the mean, N represents the total number of scores involved, and Σ (Greek capital sigma) represents "sum of" or "summation of," signifying that whatever is symbolized by the letters following it is to be added—in this case the values of X, or the measures involved.

To illustrate the application of this formula let us determine the mean of the following scores.

23	13	22	16
18	24	21	9
16	18	14	10
21	17	19	8
14	15	17	19

The sum of all 20 scores is 334. Applying the formula gives

$$M = \frac{334}{20} = 16.7$$

In any presentation on calculating the mean, books on testing commonly include a description of the procedure to be used in working with a grouped frequency distribution. However, when a teacher is computing a mean for a small number of pupils, it is much simpler to use the definition formula given above. Where greater numbers of students are involved, the increasing availability of desk-type calculators, digital computers, and test scoring and analyzing services makes it unlikely that paper-and-pencil procedures will need to be used. For these reasons, procedures for working with grouped frequency distributions are not presented in this text; they may be found in many conventional testing and statistics texts.

The Standard Deviation.   As mentioned above, the standard score describes an individual's distance from the mean in terms of the relative variability of the distribution involved. The measure of variability used for this purpose, as well as for a variety of other purposes, is the standard deviation, typically symbolized by *SD, s,* or σ (lower-case Greek sigma).

The basic formula that serves to define the standard deviation is

$$SD = \sqrt{\frac{(X - M)^2}{N}} \qquad \text{[Eq. 3]}$$

The sum to be placed in the numerator is obtained by first subtracting the mean from each score (that is, finding $X - M$ for each score), multiplying each $X - M$ value by itself to find its square, and then obtaining the sum of all such squared values. To obtain the standard deviation this sum is divided by N, and the square root of this value is then determined.

For example, let us assume that a small class of 6 students made the following scores on a quiz:

18, 15, 14, 20, 18, 11

To simplify our calculations we can arrange these scores in order of magnitude and then carry out the necessary steps for calculating the standard deviation:

X	$X - M$	$(X - M)^2$
20	4	16
18	2	4
18	2	4
15	−1	1
14	−2	4
11	−5	25
$\Sigma X = \overline{96}$		$\Sigma(X - M)^2 = \overline{54}$
$M = 16$		

$$SD = \sqrt{\frac{\Sigma(X - M)^2}{N}}$$

$$SD = \sqrt{\frac{54}{6}} = \sqrt{9}$$

$$SD = 3$$

The X column shows the 6 raw scores arranged in descending numerical order, together with the sum and the mean (M). The second column shows the deviation of each score from the mean ($X - M$), and the third column contains the square of each such deviation. As the definition formula (Equation 3) indicates, the standard deviation is calculated by dividing the sum of the squared deviations from the mean, $\Sigma(X - M)^2$, by N and then finding the square root of this result. In our example the sum of the squared deviations from the mean is equal to 54, and when this is divided by N of 6 the quotient obtained is 9. Since the square root of 9 is 3, then 3 is our standard deviation for this set of 6 scores.

The standard deviation is the most generally used measure of variability, and the test user will encounter it several times in most test manuals. Our example shows that the SD measures how much the scores in a distribution "spread out" in that the basic measure is the distance of each score from the mean. Beyond this, the reader should not expect to be able to interpret the SD in any simple absolute manner. A common error of beginning students in statistics is to try to give the SD more meaning than it actually has. When it is used to express the variability of a distribution, it can be meaningful to the extent that we can compare the SD of one distribution with that of another and thereby compare the two variabilities.

The following three points summarize what is important to remember about the standard deviation.

1. It is a measure of variability dependent on the deviation of each score from the mean.
2. It is useful as an index number for comparing the variability of two or more distributions.
3. It serves as the basic unit of measure in standard scores.

As is true with the mean and with most other statistical measures, there are a variety of essentially equivalent formulas for computing the standard deviation. Since our goal in this presentation is some understanding of the meaning of this statistic, rather than skill in computation, only Equation 3 will be presented. Persons interested in a more complete presentation of this and other measures of variability should consult a statistics text.

The Standard Score.   The basic type of standard score is generally referred to as a z-score and is defined by the following formula:

$$z = \frac{X - M}{SD}$$ [Eq. 4]

This formula tells us that the z-score corresponding to any given raw score is equal to its deviation from the mean divided by the standard deviation. Using the same distribution of scores used to illustrate the computation of the standard deviation, we can determine the z-score corresponding to each raw score:

X	X − M	z-score
20	4	1.33
18	2	.67
18	2	.67
15	−1	−.33
14	−2	−.67
11	−5	−1.67

Note that raw scores below the mean have negative z-scores. What happens when we use z-scores can be illustrated by calculating such scores for another distribution of six test scores. In this case we have made each score three times the size of the scores in the preceding distribution. The mean and standard deviation are also three times those in the first distribution; that is, $M = 48$ and $SD = 9$.

X	X − M	z-score
60	12	1.33
54	6	.67
54	6	.67
45	−3	−.33
42	−6	−.67
33	−15	−1.67

The student can check the accuracy of these figures by calculating the mean and standard deviation. It is apparent that the new distribution has a much greater variability than the preceding one, reflected both in the range between the low and high scores in each of the distributions and in the standard deviations. However, since the z-score represents the distance from the mean in terms of the relative variability of the distribution, the z-scores for the two distributions are equivalent—an illustration of how z-scores serve to make scores from the two distributions relatively equivalent even though the original distributions may differ greatly in their variabilities.

The z-score is the basic type of standard score in that it tells how far a given raw score is above or below the mean in terms of standard deviation units. However, the fact that z-scores involve negative numbers as well as fractions or decimals makes them somewhat confusing. As a result, most published tests use a standard, minor modification of the z-score. The goal in this modification is to eliminate both negative and fractional scores. The procedure used can be illustrated by an explanation of the T-score with the following formula:

$$T = 10z + 50 \qquad\qquad \text{[Eq. 5]}$$

First the z-scores are calculated, and then each z is multiplied by 10 and added to 50 to obtain the T-score. Because the result is usually rounded to the nearest whole number, multiplying by 10 eliminates the fractional numbers, while adding 50 serves to make all scores positive in value.

To understand the use of T-scores, the reader can return to our preceding distributions and note that, for a z-score of 0.67, T would equal 10×0.67 (or 6.7) + 50, or 56.7. The reported T-score would then be 57. For a negative z-score such as -1.67, the corresponding T would be determined in the same way: $10 \times (-1.67) = -16.7$, and $-16.7 + 50 = 33.3$, or 33.

Some test publishers employ the T-score as a standard score. Others use some other modification of the z-score. Some multiply each z by 20 and then add 100, while others use still different constants. The test user should consult the test manual in each case to determine the constants used in calculating standard scores. One result of all such conversions is that the multiplier becomes the standard deviation, while the constant added becomes the mean.

NORMAL DISTRIBUTION

The strengths and weaknesses of various types of derived scores can be discussed adequately only in relation to actual and theoretical distributions of test scores. The most important of the theoretical distributions is the *normal distribution.* If measures of a given physical characteristic, such as height, are obtained for a large and representative group of children of the same age, the measures for the majority of persons will be closely grouped about some "average" value, and as we move away from that average value in either a positive or negative direction we will find fewer and fewer cases. Since most physical qualities of human beings, when measured in large and unbiased samples, seem to form this rather standard type of distribution, it has come to be known as the "normal distribution." It has also been assumed that mental characteristics for any large, representative sample of subjects should form a normal distribution. As a result, most intelligence tests yield this type of distribution of measures. Hence, it can be said that intelligence, as measured by conventional intelligence tests, is approximately normally distributed in the population. As an example, we can look at the distribution of intelligence quotients for the 7273 fourth graders represented in Table 2.

TABLE 2

FREQUENCY DISTRIBUTION OF PINTNER IQ'S
FOR MODAL AGE GROUP FOR GRADE 4
METROPOLITAN NATIONAL STANDARDIZATION

IQ	f
150–59	4
140–49	11
130–39	130
120–29	662
110–19	1503
100–09	1953
90–99	1712
80–89	971
70–79	287
60–69	36
50–59	4

This frequency distribution is such that the frequencies are much larger near the center of the distribution, from 80 through 119 for example, and become steadily smaller as the IQ's depart from the average, becoming either larger or smaller. This can be seen more clearly by examining the bar graph (or histogram) for this same distribution as it is presented in Figure 20. The smooth curve that

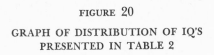

FIGURE 20

GRAPH OF DISTRIBUTION OF IQ'S
PRESENTED IN TABLE 2

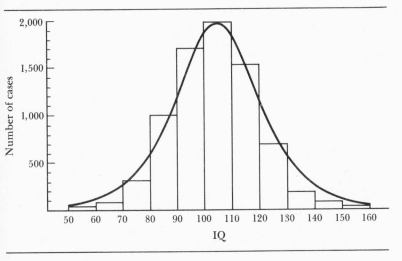

has been superimposed on the bar graph is a representation of a "normal curve" or "normal distribution" that closely approximates the actual distribution. The normal distribution is a symmetrical bell-shaped distribution, such as the one pictured here, and is defined by a specific mathematical equation.

Actual test scores are never exactly normally distributed, but they frequently approximate such a distribution. As already mentioned, this is true of the distribution of intelligence test scores for large and representative groups of persons. It is also true of scores on many achievement tests for similar large groups. The fact that such scores closely approximate a normal distribution makes it possible to use this theoretical distribution, with its known characteristics, as a basis for discussing the qualities of certain types of score. For example, it is useful in explaining a characteristic of the percentile rank scores used with many published tests.

If we were to examine a table of percentile ranks for a standardized test for which, as is typically the case, the standardization sample had scores forming an approximately normal distribution (such as shown in Figure 20), we would find that the range of scores for the top 10 percent of the group would be much greater than would be the range of scores for the middle 10 percent. That is, to include 10 percent of the persons (or of the area under the distribution curve) near the center of the distribution we would need a much shorter range along the score scale than we would if we wished to include 10 percent near one of the extremes of the distribution. As a result, distances between percentile ranks near the center of the distribution have a different meaning in terms of raw score differences than do equal distances between percentile ranks near the extremes of the distribution. This can be verified by studying the table of percentile ranks on almost any standardized test. Such a study will reveal that the difference in raw score units between the fiftieth and fifty-fifth percentiles will be much smaller than the difference between the ninetieth and ninety-fifth percentiles. That differences between percentiles have varying meanings at different points along the score scale is often cited as a weakness of the percentile rank. It might better be considered an obvious quality of such scores and one that prevents the informed test user who is aware of it from drawing unwarranted conclusions concerning the meaning of score differences.

STANINE SCORES

The stanine score, another widely used derived score, is actually based on the assumption that educational achievement is normally distributed. The meaning of these scores can be understood through reference to Figure 21. In the original development of the stanine score, the distance from a z-score of -2.75 to a z-score of 2.75 was divided into 11 equal intervals each 0.5 of a standard deviation in length, as shown in Figure 21, where the limits of the intervals are represented by such z-scores as -2.75, -2.25, -1.75, etc. The limits of the total distribution are set at -2.75 and 2.75, since essentially all (actually 99.4 percent) the area under a normal curve lies between these two points. When a normal distribution is partitioned in this way, the percentages of cases found in each interval are those shown in the first row of Figure 21. The scores falling into any given interval could then be given the number between 0 and 10 assigned to the interval, as shown in the middle row below the figure. Actually, since the percentage of cases having a score of 0 or a score of 10 on this scale is so small, and since there is some advantage (particularly when entering data on punch cards) in

FIGURE 21

GRAPH OF NORMAL DISTRIBUTION
INDICATING THE RELATIONSHIP
OF STANINE TO *z*-SCORE INTERVALS
AND PERCENTAGE OF CASES IN EACH STANINE

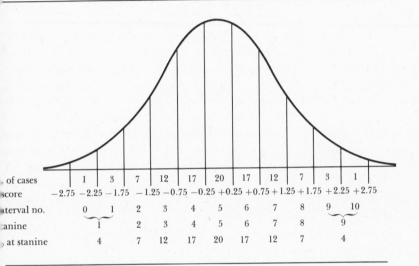

, of cases	1	3	7	12	17	20	17	12	7	3	1
score	−2.75	−2.25	−1.75	−1.25	−0.75	−0.25	+0.25	+0.75	+1.25	+1.75	+2.25	+2.75
terval no.	0	1	2	3	4	5	6	7	8	9	10
anine		1	2	3	4	5	6	7	8	9	
at stanine		4	7	12	17	20	17	12	7	4	

having only single-digit numbers as scores, the developers of the stanine scale elected to combine scores in the 0 and 1 intervals, assigning them all a stanine of 1, and to combine scores in the 9 and 10 intervals, giving them a stanine of 9. The result is that the actual scale of stanine scores and the percentage of cases included in each stanine are as shown in the last two lines of Figure 21.

It can be seen then that the stanine-score scale ranges from a low score of 1 to a high score of 9 and that the average score is 5. If further interpretation of a stanine score is necessary, use can be made of the percentage of cases at the given score and above or below it. For example, a stanine of 4 is a score slightly below the average: 17 percent of persons in the norm group make scores of this size; 23 percent make lower scores; and 60 percent make higher scores.

Since stanine scores are based on dividing the score scale into equal units (except in the cases of the first and ninth stanines), then for a distribution that is normal or assumed to be normal equal differences between stanines represent equal differences on the raw score scale.

In the treatment of stanines up to this point, we assumed a normal distribution of raw scores. What happens if a distribution is not normal? In practice, the actual computation of stanines is usually based on the percentage distribution of scores. That is, in the distribution being used as the reference group or norm group, the lowest 4 percent of the scores are given a stanine of 1, the next 7 percent a stanine of 2, the next 12 percent a stanine of 3, and so on. The result is that the transformation to stanines changes the distribution of measures into a normal distribution. The use of stanines is then based on the assumption that whatever the test is measuring actually is normally distributed and that the only reason the original raw scores are not normally distributed is that there are inadequacies in the score scale produced.

Since a stanine score can be computed rather quickly and easily on the basis of percentages, it is quite convenient to use. Some teachers convert all scores to stanines, including those from aptitude tests, from a variety of rather subjective rating devices, as well as from achievement tests. This makes possible a rather quick and simple comparison among a student's scores on all the various measures.

SUMMARY

Tests and certain other techniques enable the teacher to obtain measures of pupil achievement and other variables that are important in guiding instruction. Although the numerical results obtained in this way are not absolute or precise measures of the type obtained when a tape measure is used to determine length or distance, they do have certain qualities that make them very useful for describing student characteristics. Since a "raw score" obtained from a test has little meaning until it is compared with other scores made by other persons taking the same test, a number of "derived scores" have been developed to provide this meaning. The letter-grade may be considered a simple type of derived score. Other, more adequate scores of this type include the percentile rank, the standard score, and the stanine. The use of one of these scores in reporting and recording test results makes the results more mean-

ingful and simplifies the process of comparing a student's performance on one test with his performance on another.

Suggestions for Class Discussion and Further Investigation

1. The distribution of test scores for a large number of students
   is often organized in the form of a simple frequency distribution as shown:

Score	f	Percentile rank
40	4	
39	8	
38	11	
37	14	
36	6	
35	4	
34	2	4
33	0	2
32	1	1
	50	

   The f (or frequency) column shows how many persons made
   each raw score. Determine the percentile rank of each raw
   score using the procedure described in this chapter. (Three
   have already been computed.) Note that the numerical differences between the percentile ranks for successive raw scores
   are not equal. Why is this so? What does it show about
   percentile ranks?

2. Shown below are two hypothetical sets of test scores, "A" and
   "B," each consisting of five scores. Use the procedures described in this chapter to compute the mean and standard
   deviation for each of the two sets. Then determine the z-score
   and *T*-score corresponding to each score in each distribution.

"A"	"B"
9	28
7	24
6	22
5	20
3	16

In this case each original score in set "B" was obtained by
doubling each score in set "A" and adding 10. Note how

converting to standard scores serves to eliminate the differences between the two sets in means and standard deviations.

Suggestions for Further Reading

Rather detailed discussions of the meaning of measurement and of the problems involved in developing measuring devices in psychology and education will be found in: J. P. Guilford, *Fundamental Statistics in Psychology and Education,* 4th ed. (New York: McGraw-Hill, 1965), ch. 2; Fred N. Kerlinger, *Foundations of Behavioral Research* (New York: Holt, Rinehart and Winston, 1965), ch. 23; E. F. Lindquist, ed., *Educational Measurement* (Washington, D.C.: American Council on Education, 1951), chs. 14 and 17.

Descriptions of procedures to be used in determining the various statistical measures and scores discussed briefly in this chapter are found in a great number of available textbooks on statistics. The following represent a few of these: Robert B. Clarke, Arthur P. Coladarci, and John Caffrey, *Statistical Reasoning and Procedures* (Columbus, Ohio: Charles E. Merrill Books, 1965), chs. 1–6; William L. Hays, *Statistics for Psychologists* (New York: Holt, Rinehart and Winston, 1963), ch. 6; George H. Weinberg and John A. Schumaker, *Statistics: An Intuitive Approach* (Belmont, Calif.: Wadsworth Publishing Co., 1962), chs. 2–8.

A small but useful booklet on the use and interpretation of test scores has recently been published by the U.S. Office of Education: Kenneth F. McLauglin, *Interpretation of Test Results* (Washington, D.C.: Office of Education, U.S. Department of Health, Education, and Welfare, 1964).

Chapter Six

Using Statistics
to Appraise a Test

The preceding chapter dealt with procedures used in summarizing and analyzing test scores to obtain information about students. However, test results are also analyzed to determine certain characteristics of a test. The development of a standardized test includes its tryout with a representative sample of examinees, an analysis of such results to determine the effectiveness of individual items and of the total test, and some revision on the basis of the results. Test manuals accompanying published tests provide certain types of data that describe performance characteristics of the final form of the test.

Certain statistical procedures are used in making a test analysis. The professional teacher should have some command of these procedures to enable him to interpret data in the test manual and to apply some of these procedures to his own tests. This chapter will introduce some of the statistical analyses used for this purpose.

THE CORRELATION COEFFICIENT

In analyzing test results, a variety of questions can be answered on the basis of how one set of scores is related to another. How are pupil scores on an aptitude test related to later performance on an achievement test? Are the measures obtained from one form of a given test closely related to the results that would be obtained if a second form of the test were given to the same students? The use of the statistical technique of *correlation* provides answers to such questions. The fundamentals of this technique are illustrated by the data in Table 3.

TABLE 3

HYPOTHETICAL SCORES FOR 10 PUPILS
ON AN INTELLIGENCE TEST, A READING TEST,
AND A SCIENCE TEST

Pupil	IQ	Reading score	Science score
A	133	82	60
B	130	77	68
C	125	75	75
D	121	70	51
E	115	71	45
F	112	64	74
G	106	58	60
H	99	52	50
I	95	45	56
J	88	40	42

In this table the pupils have been arranged in descending order according to IQ's. An examination of the reading and intelligence scores shows that the pupils are ranked in about the same order on both tests. This means that there is a high correlation between intelligence quotients and reading scores. However, we do not see this same strong relationship between intelligence and science scores. In this latter case the correlation is much lower.

The relationship between two sets of paired measures can be seen more readily if the data are presented in graphic form as in Figure 22. In these graphs IQ's are measured along the horizontal axis, achievement scores along the vertical. The way in which entries are made is illustrated by the mark in Figure 22A showing the paired intelligence and reading scores for pupil *A*. This mark, in the extreme upper righthand corner of the graph, is located at the intersection of the dashed lines, one running vertically from pupil *A*'s intelligence quotient of 133, the other running horizontally from his reading score of 82. This intersection locates the point marking the paired scores for this student. The scores of all other pupils have been located in the same way.

The overall picture of the relationship in Figure 22A shows that the marks lie almost in a straight line running from the lower lefthand corner to the upper righthand corner of the graph. In contrast, the marks in Figure 22B, although showing a general trend from lower left to upper right, do not come at all close to

FIGURE 22

CORRELATION BETWEEN (A) READING AND INTELLIGENCE
AND (B) SCIENCE AND INTELLIGENCE

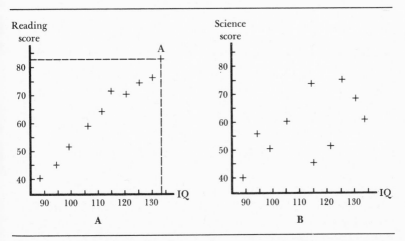

lying on one straight line. The tendency of such plotted points to lie in a straight line is a key to the concept of correlation. The closer the points come to lying in a straight line, the higher is the correlation between the two measures being studied. The extent of correlation is described by a statistical measure known as the *correlation coefficient,* generally represented by the symbol r. A perfect correlation, in which the plotted points in a graph would all fall exactly in a straight line, would yield a correlation coefficient of 1.00 ($r = 1.00$). An absolute lack of relationship would result in an r of 0.00.

Although the computation for a correlation coefficient is relatively simple and straightforward, it can be rather time-consuming if there are many scores. For this reason, and since the ability to compute a correlation coefficient contributes little to understanding it, computational procedures will not be presented here. For the beginning student in testing and measurement, the needed understanding of the concept of correlation can probably best be grasped by studying graphs or correlation charts such as those in Figure 22.

In Figure 23, four different correlation charts show the correlation coefficients resulting from different degrees of relationship as represented by plotted points for paired scores. The scatter diagram in

FIGURE 23

PLOTTED POINTS FOR PAIRED SCORES
YIELDING DIFFERENT CORRELATION COEFFICIENTS

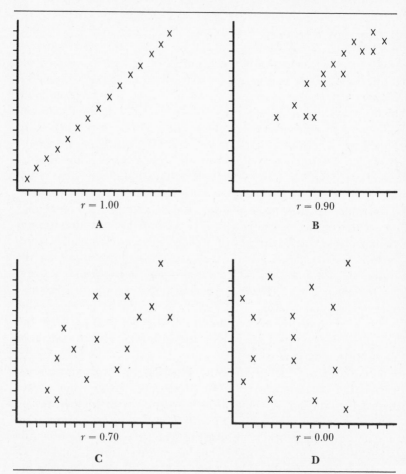

the upper lefthand corner (Figure 23A) shows that when the points lie exactly on a straight line, r will equal 1.00. Another way of illustrating perfect correlation is to note that if we knew a person's score on one measure, we could predict exactly what his score would be on the other measure. Perfect correlation permits perfect prediction. Of course, it should be added that perfect correlation ($r = 1.00$) is really never obtained in studying relationships among test scores. The complexity of the factors affecting such relationships as well as weaknesses in the measures used essentially eliminate this possibility.

Figure 23B depicts a correlation of 0.90. Where test data are involved, this would be considered a very high correlation. Here there is a tendency for the plotted points to approach a straight line pattern although they do not all lie in one line. Note, too, that such an arrangement would not permit us to tell exactly what score a pupil made on one test by knowing what he made on the other. However, since the relationship is quite strong, a prediction could be made with some accuracy. For example, if the pictured relationship were that between intelligence and reading score, such as in Figure 22, we could say such things as, "If his intelligence quotient is of this size, then we could be quite confident that his reading score would lie somewhere between this score and this score." We would make estimates, but they would include a margin of error.

When we turn to the correlation of 0.70, pictured in Figure 23C, we see that the plotted points depart much further from the straight line arrangement. There is still a general tendency for high scores on one test or measure to be associated with high scores on the other, and for low scores on one to be associated with low scores on the other. Again, if this represented the relationship between intelligence and reading achievement, it would be of some value to know a pupil's IQ if we wished to predict his reading score, but the prediction would have to be made within a rather broad range of reading scores.

Finally, Figure 23D depicts the situation in which there is no correlation whatsoever ($r = 0.00$). Here there is no tendency for high scores on one variable to be associated with high scores on the other or vice versa. A pupil with a high score on one measure might have a high score, an average score, or a low score on the other. Knowledge of a pupil's score on one test would not help us predict what he would do on the second test. In studying relationships among actual data, an r of exactly 0.00 will seldom be attained, but anything very close to this can be thought of as representing no relationship. The extremes in correlation coefficients, $r = 1.00$ and $r = 0.00$, are seldom actually obtained, but they serve to define the limits in degree of relationship, and coefficients computed from actual data take on meaning in terms of the extent to which they approach or depart from these limits.

Thus far we have considered only situations involving positive correlation—that is, situations in which high scores on one variable are associated with high scores on the other, and low scores are associated with low. It is also possible to have varying degrees of *negative correlation* if pupils getting high scores on the first test tend to get low scores on the second, while those having low scores on the first tend to get high scores on the second. This type of correlation can vary in degree of strength in the same manner as positive correlation. A perfect negative relationship is represented by an r of -1.00, which is just as valuable in predicting scores as is 1.00. Negative correlation coefficients can vary from 0.00 to -1.00. A negative correlation coefficient of -0.90 indicates as high a degree of correlation as does 0.90. Since negative correlations are seldom encountered in working with test data, the major part of our discussion has concerned positive correlation.

In studying correlation we are concerned with a procedure for examining the relationship between different sets of measures made on the same individuals. A correlation coefficient can be thought of as an index number telling us something about the strength of the relationship between two such sets of variables or telling us something about the accuracy with which we can predict one from the other. A correlation coefficient obtained in any given situation takes on meaning as we are able to compare it with others obtained in comparable circumstances. Various purposes for which correlation coefficients are used and the size of coefficient typically obtained in applying it to these purposes will be discussed in the remaining sections of this chapter.

USING CORRELATION IN DESCRIBING VALIDITY

The brief discussion of validity in chapter two defined this concept by stating that a test or other data-gathering device is *valid* to the extent that it provides the desired information concerning the examinee. Although this definition is quite simple, the problem of determining whether a test actually provides the relevant data varies from one type of test to another and can become rather complex. Methods for determining validity can be classified in four categories.

1. Content validity The assessment of this type of validity is based on a logical analysis of the relationship between the content and abilities that a test is supposed to cover and the actual content of the test items. Its most important application is with measures of achievement.

2. Concurrent validity This is determined by finding the correlation between scores on the given instrument and scores on some test or other measure administered at approximately the same time. Information concerning this type of validity is useful where one measuring device is being considered as a substitute for some other, perhaps more difficult, procedure.

3. Predictive validity This can be represented by the correlation between scores on a given instrument and measures obtained at a later time on some performance or measure that the first instrument is expected to predict. It is an important type of validity for intelligence, aptitude, and readiness tests.

4. Construct validity This is a rather complex type of validation typically used with tests measuring relatively abstract qualities, or "constructs," such as are found in the area of personality measurement. The construct validity of a test is defended by presenting data that show how certain groups of people with known characteristics differ in scores on the test or that show how these scores are related to other established measures in the same general area.

Procedures for ensuring the content validity of a test were discussed rather extensively in chapters two and three on the specification of instructional objectives and the construction of classroom tests. The description of the content validity of a test seldom involves any statistical techniques. The other three classes of validity make extensive use of statistical techniques. Because construct validity is used primarily with types of instruments not dealt with in this text, major attention will be centered on predictive and concurrent validity.

Predictive Validity. Most aptitude tests are used to predict the future performance of a pupil in some type of school work or vocational activity. To express how well scores from a given test will do this, they are correlated with measures of performance. The data used in our introductory consideration of correlation might be examples of measures used for this purpose. That is, if we wish to use intelligence test results for predicting how well pupils will do in first-grade reading, the data needed for determining the pertinent *validity coefficient* might be scores from the intelligence test administered at the start of first grade and scores from a reading achievement test administered to the same pupils at the end of first grade. The correlation between these two sets of scores would then be a validity coefficient. Since it is based on data that indicate how well the intelligence test can predict some future performance, it provides information on the *predictive validity* of the test.

For any test that is to be used for predictive purposes, the most useful information concerns its predictive validity, usually provided in the test manual of any aptitude or intelligence test. An example of data of this type is shown in Table 4.

TABLE 4

CORRELATIONS BETWEEN METROPOLITAN READINESS TESTS
AND METROPOLITAN ACHIEVEMENT TESTS

METROPOLITAN READINESS TESTS	METROPOLITAN ACHIEVEMENT TESTS	
	AVERAGE READING	NUMBERS
Test 1. Word Meaning	.409	.441
Test 2. Sentences	.418	.424
Test 3. Information	.341	.400
Test 4. Matching	.486	.541
Test 5. Numbers	.520	.634
Test 6. Copying	.341	.403
Tests 1–4. Reading Readiness	.475	.530
Tests 1–6. Total Readiness	.534	.616

* Data from Lebanon County, Pennsylvania   (Number of cases, 487)

From the Metropolitan Readiness Tests, Directions for Administering and Key for Scoring. Reproduced by permission. Copyright 1949 by Harcourt, Brace & World, Inc., New York.

In gathering data for this table, the readiness test was given in September, and the achievement test was given in the following February. The validity coefficients can be seen to vary from one type of score to another. In this particular case the most valid measure for predicting reading achievement is the total readiness score ($r = 0.534$), while the most valid predictor of numbers achievement is the numbers score on the readiness test ($r = 0.634$). All the correlation coefficients are rather modest in absolute size but are rather typical of those found in determining the predictive validity of most types of aptitude tests. We do not expect validity coefficients to be much higher than this. Knowing a test's predictive validity, the teacher with some competency in testing uses predictor tests because they can be quite helpful in determining what to expect from pupils, but he realizes that such tests will not provide an exact prediction of how well a pupil will achieve.

Information on predictive validity from a test manual is quite helpful in determining the value of a test for a particular purpose. However, when a teacher has started to use a test, he is advised to study its predictive validity in his own situation and for his own purpose. He can do this by studying the relationship between the scores his pupils make on the given predictor test and scores on some later measure of achievement. This relationship can be examined by graphing the results as illustrated in Figure 22. Studying a graph or correlation chart of this type may well be all that the teacher needs to do in examining the actual predictive validity of an instrument he is using. However, if he wishes to go further and compare the validity of the test as shown by his own data with that reported by the test publisher, he can consult a statistics textbook and actually compute a validity coefficient based on his data.

Concurrent Validity. Evidence on *concurrent validity* is obtained by comparing pupil performance on a given test with performance on some other measure obtained at essentially the same time or concurrently. Publishers of aptitude tests present information concerning concurrent validity based on a variety of other measures. They may, for example, present correlations with other aptitude tests, in which case they provide information on the extent to which their test measures the same thing as some other test. Publishers of a group intelligence test may show how scores from their test correlate with some established individual intelligence test such as the Stanford-Binet. In a sense they are saying that if one wants an instrument that measures the same thing as the Stanford-Binet test, here is evidence as to the extent to which their instrument will fill this need. To the knowledgeable test user, correlations of scores from one test with scores from other comparable well-known tests provide useful information as to what an instrument measures. Examples of data of this type are presented in Table 5. These data from the manual for the Henmon-Nelson

TABLE 5

CORRELATIONS OF HENMON-NELSON REVISION, GRADES 6-9,
WITH OTHER TESTS OF MENTAL ABILITY

Grade level	Name of other intelligence test	N	Correlation with Henmon-Nelson
9	Otis	86	0.776
7	Otis	306	0.825
9	Lorge-Thorndike	86	0.798
6	SRA Primary Mental Abilities	251	0.714
9	SRA Primary Mental Abilities	114	0.760
7	Kuhlman-Anderson	177	0.794

Adapted from Examiner's Manual, the Henmon-Nelson Tests of Mental Ability. Reprinted by permission. Copyright 1957 by Houghton Mifflin Co., Boston.

Tests of Mental Ability show the extent to which this test is measuring the same thing as several other widely used intelligence tests. Concurrent validity coefficients of this type usually will be somewhat larger than predictive validity coefficients.

Another type of concurrent validity coefficient sometimes presented with aptitude tests takes the form of correlations with scores from achievement tests taken at approximately the same time. Such coefficients should not be accepted as providing data on predictive validity. If there is no time lapse between the administration of the predictor test and the obtaining of criterion data, the relationship between the two sets of measures is not indicative of the predictive value of the test involved. A coefficient of concurrent validity obtained in this way would probably be an overestimate of the predictive validity of the test, because in actual prediction situations rather natural and expected changes in the mental and physical conditions of students from the first testing to the second testing will contribute to the lowering of the correlation and the predictive value of the test. When the predictor and the later criterion measuring device are administered concurrently, such changes are not involved, and the obtained correlation tends to be spuriously high. Concurrent validity coefficients showing the relationship between an aptitude test and some measure of achievement should be interpreted merely as indicating the extent to which the two measures are assessing the same abilities.

USING CORRELATION IN DETERMINING RELIABILITY

Reliability was described in chapter two as the extent to which a measuring procedure is capable of producing consistent results. It may also be thought of as representing the extent to which a given result represents a true measure of whatever is being assessed. A teacher interested in obtaining true measures of the weights of his pupils probably would use some type of scale that employed a balance arm and standard weights and that had been shown to produce consistent and accurate results. He would not use some procedure such as lifting each pupil himself and estimating their weights from the relative effort needed to lift them; this would result in too much error in the measure obtained for each pupil and would not lead to consistent results if a pupil were weighed more than once. If a measuring procedure is to be at all useful, it must have some degree of reliability. An intelligence test producing a given score for a pupil when administered at one particular time and yielding a quite different result when administered a few hours later would not permit us to say much about the true score for the pupil and would be of little value.

Determining Reliability. If we wish to test the reliability of a weight scale we can weigh some known weight and determine how close the reading on the scale is to the known figure. We might also weigh the same object or person over and over again and note the consistency in the results obtained. Unfortunately, neither of these procedures is usable with an educational or psychological test. There is no "true" or "standard" measure for an examinee with which we can compare an obtained test score. If there were, we probably would use this "true" measure and not worry about the estimate obtained from the actual test. Also, any typical test could not be given repeatedly to the same student because this would produce changes in the student, and successive measures of the same "thing" would not be obtained. For these reasons, the reliability of a test must be studied by means of other procedures.

The Test-Retest Procedure. A basic method for determining the reliability of a test can be thought of as being derived from the procedure of successive measures of the same thing. However, instead of testing one pupil over and over again, the method is based on only two testings of a large number of examinees. The assumption is that: (1) little change will take place in a pupil between only two successive testings, and (2) the variations between two scores for a large number of examinees will be as indicative of the inconsistencies inherent in a given procedure as will the variations among a number of scores for only one person. This procedure is known as the *test-retest procedure*.

Determining reliability through the test-retest method can be illustrated by the following example. Let us assume that we are concerned with determining the reliability of the scores from a fifty-item arithmetic computation test. We will administer this test to the appropriate group of students on some given date, and, after a few days or a few weeks, we will administer it a second time. This time lapse between the two testings should be long enough to ensure that there will be little likelihood that pupils will remember specific problems or answers, but should not be so long as to allow changes in the actual arithmetic ability of the pupils. We will obtain two independent measures of each pupil's achievement when he is at essentially the same point in his study. Although the study of the reliability of any test should be based on a minimum of from one hundred to two hundred pupils, some understanding of what is involved in this procedure can be gained by examining hypothetical scores for only a few students used in a test-retest situation. We will assume that the following scores were obtained from the two administrations of the test.

Pupil	Score on first administration	Score on second administration
A	47	48
B	46	44
C	43	42
D	38	40
E	31	36
F	36	29
G	28	30
H	27	27

We can see that the scores from the two administrations are quite similar and that there is a close relationship between the two sets of measures. To express this relationship, the correlation coefficient is computed and reported as a *coefficient of reliability*. Since this coefficient tells us something about the stability of scores over time, it is sometimes referred to as a *coefficient of stability,* which can be thought of as a specific type of reliability coefficient. Remembering our previous discussion of correlation, we can note that if the paired scores obtained from the two administrations of this test were plotted on a correlation chart, they would fall quite close to a straight line. In other words, the results from our hypothetical test-retest study would result in a fairly large correlation coefficient (the actual r here is 0.90). Actual reliability coefficients reported for most published tests are of this general magnitude. Most of the reliabilities reported in test manuals are larger than 0.80. Reliability coefficients are typically much larger than validity coefficients and a test user should question the value of scores produced by tests having reported reliabilities of less than 0.80.

The Equivalent Forms Procedure. As the reader might surmise, a difficulty in using the test-retest method of determining reliability is the possibility that a pupil's score on the second testing will be influenced by something he remembers from the first testing. This may be something as small as recalling that he made some specific guess on a particular item to which he did not know the answer. To this extent the examinee learned something from the first administration of the test, and the pupil being measured at the second testing is a changed pupil. To overcome this difficulty, a different form of the same test is used at the second testing—that is, a form of the test covering the same content with items of equal difficulty, but constructed in such a way that the recall of specific answers from the first testing cannot affect the retest score. This method of determining reliability is known as the *equivalent forms* or *alternate forms procedure.*

In using the equivalent forms procedure two different practices may be followed in timing the two administrations. In one, both forms of the test are administered at essentially the same time, one immediately following the other. Since this provides no indication of the stability of scores over time, it is almost solely a measure of the extent to which the two tests yield scores that place students in equivalent relative positions. Hence, the reliability coefficient obtained by determining the correlation between scores from the two tests is also referred to as a *coefficient of equivalence.*

The second practice allows some time interval (a few days or weeks) to elapse between the two testings. The correlation between scores obtained in this way depends both on the stability over time of the quality being measured and on the equivalence of the two forms of the test. For this reason, the reliability coefficient obtained is known as a *coefficient of stability and equivalence*. It is generally recognized that this latter procedure provides the most rigorous estimate of the reliability of a test.

The coefficients of stability, of equivalence, and of stability and equivalence are all coefficients of reliability. We have described these different forms of reliability coefficients in order to emphasize some of the factors of inconsistency in scores derived by each of the various methods. Reliability coefficients reported in test manuals will generally be identified as coefficients of reliability, and the reader must determine for himself whether the method used involves equivalence, stability, or both.

An example of alternate forms reliability data as reported in a test manual is given in Table 6. The manual reports that there was a time interval of from four to ten days between first and second testings. Note that the group was divided so that some pupils took Form A first and some took Form B first. It can be seen

TABLE 6

ALTERNATE FORMS RELIABILITY COEFFICIENTS
WITH MEANS AND STANDARD DEVIATIONS
FOR RAW SCORES ON FORMS A AND B, GRADES 6–9,
FOR THE HENMON-NELSON TESTS OF MENTAL ABILITY

| N (Grade 6) | Raw Scores | | | | *r* |
| | Form A | | Form B | | |
	Mean	Standard Deviation	Mean	Standard Deviation	
126 (Form A taken first; Form B, second)	52.58	12.90	57.00	11.03	.865
89 (Form B taken first; Form A, second)	54.28	12.92	53.75	11.93	.901

that the two reliability coefficients obtained are well above 0.80. Attention should also be given to the means and standard deviations for the two groups on the two tests. These are quite similar except for the slightly higher mean on Form B for the first group.

The Split-Halves Procedure. In the equivalent forms procedure for determining reliability, the forms may be thought of as being made up of samples of items drawn from a common pool of items that can be used in testing in the given area. What might be considered a modification of this procedure is the *split-halves procedure* in which one test is thought of as being split in two and each half is a sample of possible test items. The correlation between scores from the two halves then yields something comparable to a co-efficient of equivalence. However, the coefficient obtained in this way represents the reliability of a test that is only half as long as the actual test, and the coefficient must be modified if it is to be taken as an estimate of reliability.

The usual procedure in applying the split-halves method is to give the test in question only once. After the responses have been marked correct or incorrect, two separate scores are recorded for each paper. One score represents the total of odd-numbered items answered correctly; the other represents the total of correct even-numbered answers. That is, the test is considered as being split so that the odd-numbered items make up one half and the even-numbered items the other. This specific method is described as the *odd-even split-halves procedure.*

As indicated previously, the correlation between scores on odd-numbered items and scores on even-numbered items, or between any two halves of a test, is a measure of the equivalence of two tests each of which is only half as long as the actual test. Since a shorter test, giving a less adequate sample of an examinee's ability, can be expected to be less reliable than a longer one, a standard formula is applied to the correlation between the two halves in order to raise it so that it represents an adequate estimate of the reliability of the full-length test. This is the Spearman-Brown prophecy or correction formula and can be represented as follows:

$$\text{split-halves reliability coefficient} = \frac{2r_{hh}}{1 + r_{hh}}$$

Here r_{hh} represents the original correlation between the two halves. To illustrate the application of the formula, let us assume that the correlation between two halves of a test is found to be 0.70. The Spearman-Brown formula would then be applied as follows:

$$\text{split-halves reliability coefficient} = \frac{2 \times 0.70}{1 + 0.70} = \frac{1.4}{1.7} = 0.82$$

The split-halves reliability coefficient would then be reported as 0.82.

Table 7 provides an example of actual split-halves reliability

TABLE 7

ODD-EVEN RELIABILITY
OF LORGE-THORNDIKE INTELLIGENCE TESTS

Battery and Level	Grade Level	No. of Cases	Raw Score		Correlation (Corrected)
			Mean	S.D.	
PRIMARY					
Level 1	Kg	295	32.86	10.70	.916
Level 2	2	138	46.34	5.38	.586*
NONVERBAL					
Level 3	5	152	52.61	12.51	.940
Level 4	8	199	46.52	12.79	.928
Level 5	11	144	45.02	11.08	.905
VERBAL					
Level 3	5	163	58.13	13.85	.940
Level 4	8	192	50.10	13.26	.929
Level 5	11	153	48.91	12.97	.882

* At this level, an *odd-even* reliability coefficient is not really meaningful, since there is a systematic alternation between geometric and pictorial items in subtests 2 and 3.

From Technical Manual, The Lorge-Thorndike Intelligence Tests. Reproduced by permission. Copyright 1957 by Houghton Mifflin Co., Boston.

data. Note that with these tests all the reliability coefficients are in the high 0.80's or low 0.90's, with the exception of the one very low coefficient explained in the footnote.

Internal Consistency Reliability. We have seen that the split-halves procedure actually tells something about the extent to which one half of a test is equivalent to the other half. It can also provide information concerning the "internal consistency" of a test. Another procedure for determining reliability that is frequently used with published tests and that provides information on the internal consistency of a test is the Kuder-Richardson procedure. The various means for computing a reliability coefficient used with this general procedure are too complex to be explained here. The beginner in testing can perhaps understand the meaning of a Kuder-Richardson reliability coefficient most easily if he interprets such a coefficient as representing the average of all the split-halves coefficients that could be determined for a given test.

Standard Error of Measurement. Another statistical measure used in describing the reliability of a test is the *standard error of measurement.* In introducing the concept of reliability we suggested that one conceivable means of describing it would be to measure the same thing many times and note how much all these measures vary from one another. The standard error of measurement provides evidence of this type. If a test could be given over and over again to a student (without changing his ability with respect to the quality being measured), the standard deviation of this distribution of actual scores for one person would be represented by the standard error of measurement. Of course, because it is not possible to continue retesting persons in this way without changing them, the standard error of measurement is not determined by actual trial, but is estimated by using the formula

$$SE_{meas} = SD\sqrt{1 - r_{tt}}$$

where *SD* represents the standard deviation of scores from the test in question and r_{tt} represents its reliability.

The standard error of measurement is to be thought of as telling something about how close an actual score approximates a person's theoretical true score. The usual way of explaining it is to assume that any person's hypothetical distribution of actual scores is normally distributed and to state that 68 percent of the time a person's actual score is within a distance of one standard error of measurement of his true score. Hence, the standard error of measurement provides information as to the accuracy of the scores yielded by a test. As with many other statistics, however, it is most easily used for purposes of comparison. That is, if two tests are considered for use, one way of comparing the accuracy with which they measure is to compare their standard errors of measurement.

OTHER USES OF CORRELATION

The two most important purposes for which correlation coefficients are used in describing a test are expressing validity and reliability. However, test manuals sometimes use such coefficients to present other types of information.

Correlation of Items with Total Score.   It is possible to compute a correlation coefficient that expresses the relationship between how well a person performs on any individual test item and his score on the total test. This coefficient provides some information concerning the extent to which an item measures the same type of thing as the total test. If all such item-test correlations are quite high for a given test the test is said to be quite *homogeneous* in that all items appear to be related to the same ability. Information of this type is sometimes obtained for a preliminary form of a test and is used to eliminate those items that are not to be used in the finished version. Data on the average correlation between individual test items and total test score are sometimes presented as information about the validity of a test. This is essentially a misrepresentation of these data and can be misleading to the uninformed or partially informed person. An instrument may have a high average item-test correlation and be quite poor in its content, concurrent, predictive, or construct validity.

Correlations Among Subtests.   Many tests actually comprised of a number of discrete subtests, each yielding a separate score, include data in the manual showing the intercorrelations among the subtests. Such correlations are particularly meaningful where the various subtests are supposed to measure different abilities and to be useful for diagnostic purposes. An example of information of this type is presented in Table 8. The first coefficient in the table (0.11) shows the correlation between the rate score and the comprehension score. The extremely low correlation tells us that there is essentially no relationship between a pupil's rate of reading and his performance on the comprehension test. This suggests that these are separate abilities and must each be measured if we are to get

TABLE 8

INTERCORRELATIONS OF SUBTEST RAW SCORES
AND THEIR CORRELATION WITH
THE MEDIAN STANDARD SCORES ON THE TOTAL TEST
FOR 173 PUPILS IN GRADE 10, NEWTON, N.J.

TEST	1R	1C	2	3	4	5	6	7A	7B
1: Rate									
1: Comprehension	.11								
2: Directed Reading	.27	.28							
3: Poetry Compre-									
hension	.30	.22	.38						
4: Word Meaning	.29	.52	.49	.45					
5: Sentence Meaning	.06	.49	.36	.25	.57				
6: Paragraph Com-									
prehension	.30	.37	.51	.46	.61	.48			
7A: Use of Index	.10	.30	.45	.32	.47	.29	.41		
7B: Selection of Key									
Words	.10	.32	.30	.26	.36	.36	.37	.27	
Median Standard									
Score	.39	.57	.63	.59	.81	.63	.75	.61	.50

From Iowa Silent Reading Tests, Advanced Test: Manual of Directions. Reproduced by permission. Copyright 1927, 1931, 1939, 1943
by Harcourt, Brace & World, Inc., New York.

a total picture of a pupil's overall reading ability. Data of this
type, showing the degree of independence of subtests in a battery,
are provided with many published tests and furnish meaningful
information concerning the test scores.

SUMMARY

It is sometimes said that "a test is known by its correlations." Although many important things about a test cannot be studied
through the use of any type of statistical analysis, much can be
learned about it by studying certain correlations. In investigating
the concurrent and the predictive validity of an instrument, one
can determine its correlation with certain criterion measures.
Studying its reliability through the use of such standard procedures
as (1) test-retest, (2) alternate forms, and (3) split-halves techniques
requires the determination of the correlation between comparable
measures. Also, in many cases useful information is provided in
the form of correlations between performance on individual items
and score on the total test and in the form of intercorrelations
among subtests making up a test battery. Some basic understanding
of the concept of correlation and its many applications in the

appraisal of the qualities of a test is essential for anyone who aspires to any degree of competency in measurement and evaluation.

Suggestions for Class Discussion and Further Investigation

1. Re-examine Table 4 and Figure 24 and notice the differences in the size of the validity coefficients reported. What reasons can you give as to why the coefficients reported in Table 4 are so much larger?
2. For each of the following questions decide which type of validity or reliability is of concern to the questioner. Explain what type of evidence could best be used to answer the question.
   a. Will my students show about the same IQ's from this test if I give it today as they will if I give it next week?
   b. Will this test, if given at the start of the term, give me some idea as to how well the students will do on the final examination for this course?
   c. Can I use this test to compare the achievement of last year's class with that of this year's class even though I gave Form A of the test last year and Form B this year?
   d. Would this aptitude test be useful for dividing my class into slow, average, and fast groups before beginning reading instruction?
3. List all the things that you can think of that might make an equivalent forms reliability coefficient (coefficient of stability and equivalence) lower than a split-halves reliability coefficient for the same test.

Suggestions for Further Reading

Presentations on the computation and use of the correlation coefficient can be found in most elementary statistics textbooks. The following are a few examples of such sources: Robert B. Clark, Arthur P. Coladarci, and John Caffrey, *Statistical Reasoning and Procedures* (Columbus, Ohio: Charles E. Merrill Books, 1965), ch. 7; J. P. Guilford, *Fundamental Statistics in Psychology and Education,* 4th ed. (New York: McGraw-Hill, 1965), ch. 6; Helen M. Walker and Joseph Lev, *Elementary Statistical Methods,* rev. ed. (New York: Holt, Rinehart and Winston, 1958), chs. 9–11; George H. Weinberg and John A. Schumaker, *Statistics: An Intuitive Approach* (Belmont, Calif.: Wadsworth Publishing Co., 1962), chs. 16–18.

Rather extensive discussions of the topics of validity and reliability will be found in: Lee J. Cronbach, *Essentials of Psychological Testing*, 2nd ed. (New York: Harper & Row, 1960), chs. 5–6; Fred N. Kerlinger, *Foundations of Behavioral Research* (New York: Holt, Rinehart and Winston, 1965), chs. 24–25; E. F. Lindquist, ed., *Educational Measurement* (Washington, D.C.: American Council on Education, 1951), chs. 15–16.

Chapter Seven

Standardized Achievement Tests

For the important task of evaluating the extent to which pupils have achieved the objectives of instruction, the most useful and valid devices are those produced by a teacher to meet the needs of his particular situation. Teacher-made tests can assess the abilities outlined in the specific objectives for a course, thus providing the teacher with essential information about pupil mastery of these abilities. In this sense they provide "content-referenced" measures.

At times, however, it is useful for a teacher, a pupil, or a parent to know how the achievement of pupils in a given school compares with the achievement of their peers in other schools. Are the pupils in this fourth grade class doing as well in arithmetic computation as are pupils in typical fourth grade classes? Is their reading comprehension as good? Answers to such questions may be important in evaluating the effectiveness of an instructional program or in comparing the relative proficiencies of students. Standardized achievement tests help to provide such answers.

As is true of many concepts, the meaning of the term "standardized test" can be fully understood only after one has become familiar with such tests and has used them for a variety of purposes. However, it is useful to start our study of such instruments with a delineating definition or description. *A standardized test is a published test, accompanied by specific directions for administering and scoring, that has been given to a representative group of subjects so that the performance of any examinee can be compared with the performance of typical examinees through the use of derived scores or norms.* This chapter will enlarge on this definition by explaining how these tests are developed, providing descriptions of a few representative tests, and offering suggestions for their selection and use.

THE DEVELOPMENT OF A STANDARDIZED ACHIEVEMENT TEST

The task of developing a standardized achievement test for general use is a lengthy process involving many steps and the work of many persons.

Planning and Writing the Initial Version.   As in the development of teacher-made tests, the first step in the construction of a standardized test is the determination of what the instrument shall measure. Obviously, the general area with which the test is concerned is determined by the interests of the author or the desires of the publisher. Some tests are limited to one subject such as reading, arithmetic, chemistry, or world history. Others are test batteries, made up of subtests in many content areas. Decisions must be made concerning the exact content and abilities to be covered within the subject area and grade level for which the test is intended.

Test authors and publishers vary greatly in the care with which they describe in their test manuals what their instruments are designed to measure. Some present a detailed outline showing the plan on which the selection of content was based. Others provide only a few descriptive statements. Some test authors determine the basic content of their tests by surveying the textbooks most widely used for that particular subject and by analyzing course outlines followed by some of the larger school systems. In general, test producers try to develop tests that cover the material studied in typical school systems. They do not attempt to set the pace by suggesting what content the pupils should master; instead they endeavor to construct tests that are useful to, and hence salable to, a large portion of the nation's schools.

An author's statement of what the test is intended to measure should not be accepted as the final word on what it actually does measure. The user can determine this only after a careful examination of the test items themselves. However, the test producer's description or outline will be a useful aid in determining just what the instrument assesses.

Planning for the test also requires decisions other than those involving content. Additional points to be decided include the number and types of items to be used and the relative emphasis to be placed on the different abilities listed in the outline of content. When all such issues have been settled, the actual writing of items begins. This may be done by one person who is quite competent both in the content being covered and in techniques of item-writing. More frequently, however, it is a team effort, including some persons with strong subject-matter competencies and others with a major proficiency in test construction. In any case, the effort typically involves considerable consultative and editorial assistance, provided by experienced staff members of the test publisher.

The Item Analysis Program.   When a preliminary version of the standardized test, which includes many more items than are needed for the final version, has been prepared, it is administered to a relatively large group of students who are judged to be representative of persons for whom the test is intended. This group need not be as large nor as truly representative as that used in the standardization of the final form of the test, since it is used only to determine the relative effectiveness of the original items. However, if the item analysis program is to be meaningful, the group must consist of pupils who are typical of those who will be using the completed test. Detailed information on each pupil's performance is summarized to indicate each item's *discriminating capacity* and *difficulty*.

1. *Discriminating capacity*   If a test item is to provide valid information and contribute to the overall validity of a test, it must discriminate between persons who have the ability that the item is intended to measure and persons who do not. Test producers use two procedures to estimate the extent to which an item has this capacity for discrimination. One is to determine the percentage of students who pass the item at each of several successive grade levels. If, for example, it is found that an item is passed by 23 percent of third graders, 41 percent of fourth graders, 53 percent of fifth graders, and 71 percent of six graders, it obviously measures something on which students become more proficient as they progress through these grades. If an item does not show a pattern of increase in correct responses with an increase in grade level, it is probably a poor item in which some extraneous factor, such as

guessing, is playing a major part, or it may be measuring something pupils do not become more proficient at as they progress. In any case, the item probably would be discarded or rewritten.

Another procedure commonly used to determine discriminating capacity is to compute the correlation between passing or failing the item and the total score on the test, based on the assumption that pupils with high total test scores are good students with respect to the overall content of the test whereas those with low scores are poor students. An item is judged to be discriminating, then, if it is passed by a higher percentage of good students than poor students. One rather standard procedure employed is to select the upper 27 percent of test papers, in terms of total score, and to use these as representing "good" students and the bottom 27 percent of the papers as representing "poor" students. For each item the percentage of "good" students and the percentage of "poor" students passing it are determined. Data of this type for a few hypothetical items could be represented as follows:

	Percentage passing item	
	Good students	Poor students
item 1	70	32
item 2	94	56
item 3	29	33
item 4	47	18

These data would indicate that item 1 is of average difficulty and discriminates quite well between good and poor students. Item 2 is easy but still discriminating. Item 3, with nearly equal percentages passing among good and poor students, does not help to discriminate between these two groups. Item 4 is evidently quite difficult but discriminating. With this information, the test producer might well retain items 1, 2, and 4. Item 3 will be either discarded or, if it deals with some essential content, rewritten to correct for its lack of discriminating capacity and given another trial.

There is no simple, set standard for deciding whether a test item displays an adequate discriminating capacity. The problem of developing discriminating items is simpler in some subject-matter areas than in others. Usually a test producer will weigh information on discriminating capacity along with data on item difficulty and information concerning the importance of the content covered and will then select or reject items on the basis of all these criteria.

Other things being equal, he will select the items that show the greatest discriminating power.

Teachers will probably find it useful to gather information, such as the type suggested above, about the discriminating capacities of their own test items. This frequently provides some insights into their capabilities at item-writing as well as the effectiveness of their instruction. However, such data should not be taken as absolute authority as to the worth of an item, but merely as interesting data that should be considered along with other information.

2. Item difficulty Information about item difficulty is important for (1) making certain that a final version of a test consists of items with a suitable range of difficulty, (2) balancing alternate forms with respect to this quality, and (3) arranging items within a test in an approximate order of increasing difficulty. It is usually expressed merely in terms of percentage of persons answering the item correctly. From results obtained in this way, items that are too difficult or too easy are discarded or rewritten. A typical goal is to choose items with an average difficulty of somewhere between 50 and 65 percent passing.

Some actual data on item difficulty for one of the subtests on the Iowa Tests of Basic Skills are presented in Table 9. Not all items have been taken by pupils at all grade levels, but there is some overlapping from grade to grade. A close study of the table tells us, for example, that item 31 was passed by 32 percent of third graders, 60 percent of fourth graders, and 68 percent of fifth graders. Note that the items included at each grade level have an average difficulty level of about 60 percent and that the range in difficulty of items is approximately the same within all grades.

The reader should also find it interesting to examine Table 9 in terms of the discriminating capacity of various items, by percentage passing at each grade level. This has already been seen in the case of item 31. As another example, the table tells us that item 30 was passed by 34 percent of third graders, 58 percent of fourth graders, and 72 percent of fifth graders. Both items 30 and 31, then, seem to possess satisfactory discriminating capacity in terms of the criterion of increasing percentage of correct responses with increase in grade.

This description of item analysis procedures has touched briefly on the principal techniques employed for this purpose. The student who wishes to become more fully informed on this topic

TABLE 9

DISTRIBUTIONS OF ITEM DFFICULTY INDEXES
FOR TEST L–1, SPELLING, FORM 2

	Grade 3	Grade 4	Grade 5	Grade 6	Grade 7	Grade 8
.98						
96						
94						
92						
90						
88						
86						
84	3	11	26		59	
82	1 2		24 36			
80		13	29 35	40 55		69 72
78	7	15		41 42	60 65	67 70
76	5 9	12 14	25 27 40	43	58 62	74 75
74	4		55	45	63	68 71 73 77 82 93
72	8	17 24 26	30	44 59	66 68 69 72	78 85
70	10 11 26	18 20	41 42	49	61 64 67 82	83
68	6	25	28 31 32 44 45	68		76 79 95
66	12 13	22	33	47 61 62	70 71	80 81 87 99
64		19 23 27 29	43	50 60 69	74	
62		·21 41	34	46 58 67 72	73 75 76 79 85	
60	14 15 17 24	16 31 36	37 39 49	63 65 71	77 78	84 89
58	19	30	38	48 51 54 57		88 92 107
56	16 18 25	32 33 42	46 58 59 61		83	86 90
54		34 35	48	53 70 73	80 81 93	98 105 111
52		37	47 60	52 64 66 74		
50		40	50 62 65	56 75 82		97 101 104 106
48	20	28	52	76 83	84	91 100
46	27	38 43 44	51 54 64	77 79	86 99	96 108
44	21 22		53 63		88	94 102 103
42		39 45		81	89 97	
40	29			78 80 84	87 90 96 98	109 110
38				85	91 94 95	
36	23 28					
34	30	47	56		92 100	113
32	31	46	66		101	112 114
30		48	57		102 103 104 105	
28						
26	·					
24						
22						
20						
18						
16						
14						
12						
10						
8						
6						
4						
2						

From the Manual for the Iowa Tests of Basic Skills. Reproduced by permission.
Copyright 1956 by the State University of Iowa, Houghton Mifflin Co., Boston.

should study the descriptions of specific procedures in the manuals of published achievement tests.

After the item analysis has been made the test producers, using this information together with the original plans and specifications for the test, assemble the items into the final form, or multiple equivalent forms, of the test. Then, detailed directions for administering and scoring are prepared, and the test is ready for standardization.

The Standardization Program.   An essential quality of a standardized test is that it provides a means of comparing the performance of pupils in any one school or classroom with that of "typical" pupils. The procedure that yields results making this type of comparison possible is referred to as *standardization.*

To standardize a test, it is administered to a large group of students generally representative of the grade and age levels for which it is intended. This group is typically denoted as the *standardization sample* or *norm sample.* The extent to which it is truly representative of any particular population varies greatly from test to test. In some cases a major effort is made to see that the sample is representative of all pupils in the country. In other cases a much more modest sample is taken.

An example of one of the more ambitious efforts in obtaining a standardization sample is the procedure that was used with the Iowa Tests of Basic Skills. The goal was to obtain samples from schools in all geographical regions of the country and in communities of all size classifications. Table 10 provides data showing, within each geographical region, the percentage of pupils coming from each size of community. A comparison of these data with a table showing what percentage of the total population in each region is found in communities of each size shows that, with a few exceptions, the percentages shown here are quite representative of the population. The manual for the test also provides information indicating that for the sample the overall percentages of students from each geographic region are very close to the percentage distribution figures for the total population.

For every standardized test, the manual or some other publication made available by the test producer provides a description of the composition of the standardization sample for that test. The potential user of a test should always examine these descriptions

TABLE 10

DISTRIBUTION OF PUPILS
IN THE STANDARDIZATION SAMPLE
AMONG VARIOUS SIZED COMMUNITIES

Region	Per Cent of Regional Samples Living in Various Sized Communities					
	100,000 and Over	50,000– 99,999	25,000– 49,999	10,000– 24,999	5,000– 9,999	Rural and Under 5,000*
New England	28%	16%	13%	10%	7%	26%
Middle Atlantic	44	7	7	10	7	25
East North Central	34	7	9	9	22	19
West North Central	26	6	5	10	10	43
South Atlantic	13	6	5	7	7	62
South Central	0	22	21	5	5	47
Mountain	20	7	9	9	9	46
Pacific	41	12	3	12	5	27
Total U. S.	25	11	8	9	9	38

* Includes pupils in rural schools, consolidated or union schools in rural areas, and schools located in rural communities of fewer than 5,000 inhabitants.

From the Manual for the Iowa Tests of Basic Skills. Reproduced by permission. Copyright 1956 by the State University of Iowa, Houghton Mifflin Co., Boston.

to determine whether it would be meaningful to compare his students with the specific norm sample.

When the test has been administered to the norm sample, the test producer has information from which he can compute various types of scores or *norms*—that is, derived scores that permit an easy comparison of the performance of any pupil who will later take the test with the performance of "typical" pupils as represented by the standardization or norm sample. Typical norms produced in this way are *standard scores, percentile ranks, stanine scores, grade equivalents,* and *age equivalents.* The procedure for derivation and some explanation of the meaning of each type of score is presented in the following sections.

Types of Norm. Almost all standardized tests provide for reporting scores in a number of different forms, thus permitting the test user to select the score or scores which will be most useful for his particular purpose. Since not all tests provide exactly the same types of scores or norms, one of the things which should be determined before a test is adopted is whether or not it provides those scores or norms which will be most useful for the particular testing purpose. The norms described below include those which are most commonly found on standardized achievement tests.

1. Standard scores   Chapter five presents a rather full discussion of standard scores which the reader might wish to review. Standard scores are seldom used in explaining pupil performance either to pupils or to parents because other types of norms are more easily understood. The test user will find, however, that with many tests a first step in converting from raw scores to other types of measure is to translate raw scores to standard scores, usually through a simple conversion table. These standard scores are then used in reading various tables to determine other norms. Standard scores are also regularly used in analyzing test results for research purposes. The particular qualities of standard scores, as discussed in previous sections, make them particularly useful for such purposes.

2. Percentile (or centile) ranks   Norms in terms of percentile ranks are provided with most standardized tests and are meaningful if used appropriately. Table 11 provides an example of a norm table used in deriving percentile ranks. The person scoring the tests would obtain the raw score for a student from the test itself, locate that score, or the one closest to it, in the proper column in the body of the table, and then look at the marginal columns to determine the percentile rank for the particular person. For example, a college girl's raw score of 58 would give her a percentile rank of 75. For raw scores that fall at some point between those actually listed in the table, a simple process of interpolation is used. For example, a college girl's raw score of 59, falling midway between the two listed scores of 58 and 60, would result in a percentile rank of 77.5, midway between the 75 and 80 associated with the two listed raw scores. Fractional scores are rounded to the nearest whole number (78 in this case).

In using a table of percentile ranks, the teacher should keep in mind certain characteristics of these scores.

1. A student's percentile rank tells what percentage of persons in a particular norm sample had raw scores lower than his. The percentile ranks in Figure 30, for example, tell what percentage of males and what of females in a particular college norm sample had scores below those listed. With most tests used in the elemen-

TABLE 11

SUPPLEMENTARY COLLEGE NORMS:
SELECTED PERCENTILE RANKS CORRESPONDING
TO QUICK WORD TEST RAW SCORES, LEVEL 2,
AND SUMMARY STATISTICS

%ile Rank	QUICK WORD TEST LEVEL 2 RAW SCORES			%ile Rank
	College Males	College Females	Total	
98	82	77	80	98
95	76	72	74	95
90	70	66	68	90
85	66	63	65	85
80	63	60	62	80
75	61	58	59	75
70	58	55	57	70
65	56	53	55	65
60	54	51	53	60
55	52	49	51	55
50	50	48	49	50
45	48	46	47	45
40	46	44	45	40
35	44	42	43	35
30	42	40	41	30
25	40	38	39	25
20	37	36	36	20
15	34	33	34	15
10	31	30	31	10
5	26	26	26	5
2	21	22	22	2
Number	648	539	1,187	
Mean	51.0	48.1	49.7	
S.D.	14.8	13.9	14.5	
KR_{21}	.90	.88	.89	
S.E.$_{meas.}$	4.7	4.8	4.8	

Note: The Supplementary College Norms groups were predominantly upper division sociology students tested in the spring semester.

From Borgatta-Corsini, *Quick Word Test Manual*. Reproduced by permission. Copyright 1964 by Harcourt, Brace & World, Inc., New York.

tary and secondary schools, the percentile norms are based on pupils at specific grade levels.

2. As with any type of test score, these scores have a certain degree of unreliability and must not be given too exact an interpretation. For example, if one pupil earns a percentile rank of 56 and another a percentile rank of 54 on the same test, this should not be taken as conclusive evidence that the first pupil is superior to the second. Scores are to be taken only as estimates of a pupil's standing and must not be viewed as exact measures that permit such fine discriminations. To emphasize this point, some test publishers report "percentile bands" rather than exact percentile ranks for raw scores. A portion of a table for a test which uses this procedure is shown in Table 12. Note that for given scores (in this case, converted from original raw scores) an interval rather than a spe-

TABLE 12

INDIVIDUAL SCORE NORMS FOR STEP READING,
GRADES 7, 8, AND 9, FALL TESTING

Converted Score	Grade 7	Percentile Band Grade 8	Grade 9
306-307			98 -100
304-305			96 -100
302-303	97-100	97-100	92 -100
300-301	96-100	96- 99.8	89 - 99
298-299	94-100	94- 99.3	87 - 98
296-297	92- 99.3	91- 99	82 - 96
294-295	90- 99	88- 98	77 - 94
292-293	86- 97	85- 96	71 - 91
290-291	85- 96	82- 94	65 - 87
288-289	80- 94	77- 91	61 - 82
286-287	78- 92	73- 88	56 - 77
284-285	74- 90	70- 85	51 - 71
282-283	70- 86	65- 82	47 - 65
280-281	67- 85	61- 77	43 - 61
278-279	63- 80	55- 74	37 - 58
276-277	61- 78	53- 72	35 - 53
274-275	54- 76	45- 70	29 - 51
272-273	52- 72	42- 65	27 - 47

From *STEP Manual for Interpreting Scores, Reading.* Reproduced by permission. Copyright 1957, Cooperative Test Division, Educational Testing Service, Princeton, New Jersey.

cific percentile rank is reported. This interval is known as a *percentile band*. For example, a person whose converted score was 294 would have a percentile band of 90–99. This means that, although the reliability of the test is such that this student cannot be assigned any one percentile rank as his exact "true score," we can be quite confident that his "true score" lies somewhere between 90 and 99. As explained in the *Manual for Interpreting Scores* for this particular test, STEP Reading:

> If the test interpreter assumes that students' "true" standings lie somewhere within the percentile bands corresponding to their obtained scores, in the long run he will be correct in his assumption about 68 percent of the time.[1]

It should be emphasized that percentile ranks are no more unreliable than are any other type of score and that it would be quite reasonable to provide "bands" rather than exact scores for all types of norm.

3. Equal differences between percentile ranks do not necessarily represent equal differences in raw scores. This characteristic, discussed in some detail in the presentation on the percentile rank in chapter five, is illustrated by the data in Table 11. Note, for example, that for college males, the ninetieth percentile is 70 and the ninety-fifth is 76. A difference of 5 points in percentile ranks is associated with a difference of 6 points in raw scores. Now, move down the scale and note that the difference between the fifty-fifth and sixtieth percentiles equals only 2 points, the difference between raw scores of 52 and 54. A further study of such differences will reveal a characteristic of any table of percentile ranks based on a standardization sample that is anywhere near a normal distribution: between successive fifth percentiles the raw score differences will be quite small near the center of the distribution and will increase in size as they move toward either extreme.

If the cautions suggested above are kept in mind, the percentile rank can be a very useful type of norm for the classroom teacher. It is quite simple to explain to pupils and to parents. Also, since it reports the student's standing in relationship to other pupils at his own level in school, it makes clear that, even though his score may be quite high or low, there are other pupils at his level who are scoring above and below him. It does not suggest, as such

---

1. *STEP Manual for Interpreting Scores, Reading.*

scores as grade equivalents or age equivalents might, that he is entirely out of step with other pupils at his school level.

3. *Stanine scores*   The basis for the derivation of stanine scores was explained in chapter five. As indicated in that discussion, stanine scores have the virtues of involving single-digit numbers only, of having approximately equal units at all points along the scale, and of not implying a greater exactness in measurement than is warranted.

Published tests that provide stanine score norms present them in tables showing the stanine equivalents for raw or standard scores. An example of such a table is provided in Table 13.

TABLE 13

MIDDLE-OF-YEAR STANINES
CORRESPONDING TO
METROPOLITAN STANDARD SCORES, GRADE 9

STA-NINE	AGE–CONTROLLED			
	1 Read-ing	2 Spell-ing	3 Lan-guage	4 Lang. St. Sk.
9	72–above	72–above	72–above	75–above
8	65–71	65–71	65–71	68–74
7	59–64	59–64	59–64	60–67
6	52–58	52–58	52–58	53–59
5	45–51	44–51	45–51	45–52
4	38–44	37–43	38–44	38–44
3	30–37	30–36	31–37	31–37
2	23–29	23–29	23–30	23–30
1	22–below	22–below	22–below	22–below

From Metropolitan Achievement Tests, High School Battery, Language Tests, *Manual of Directions.* Reproduced by permission. Copyright 1962, 1964 by Harcourt, Brace & World, Inc., New York.

Suggestions as to how stanines may be interpreted can be gained from Figure 24. This shows the percentage of persons at each stanine and, as shown by the percentile rank of each dividing point between stanines given in the bottom line, the percentage of persons scoring below each stanine. These can be useful in explaining what any given stanine means. For more general explanations, use can be made of the qualitative descriptions given at the top of the graph.

FIGURE 24

STANINE SCALE FOR A NORMAL DISTRIBUTION

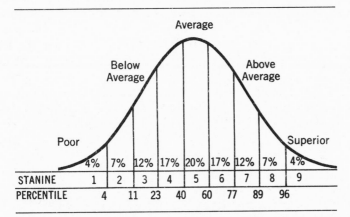

From Stanford Achievement Test, Primary II Battery, *Directions for Administering*. Reproduced by permission. Copyright 1964 by Harcourt, Brace & World, Inc., New York.

4. Grade equivalents A widely used score for standardized achievement tests is the grade equivalent, which attempts to represent a person's test performance in terms of the grade level of the students for whom it would be typical. The procedure for developing such scores involves giving the test to groups of students at various specific grade levels and then finding the average score for each group. This score is then assigned a grade equivalent equal to the grade placement of the group. The procedure can be illustrated by reference to Table 14.

Table 14 provides both grade and age equivalents for a person's median score on several subtests of the Iowa Silent Reading Test. Note, too, that this is a case in which raw scores are first converted to standard scores before this norm table can be used. If we assume that this test was given to a group of pupils who were just starting the second grade (grade placement 2.0), we see that the average standard score for this group was 104. As a result, the median standard score of 104 has a grade equivalent of 2.0. Of course, the test has not been given to groups at all grade placement levels represented by the listed grade equivalents. Typically, a test is given to pupils at varying specific levels and the grade equivalents for

TABLE 14

GRADE AND AGE EQUIVALENTS
CORRESPONDING TO MEDIAN STANDARD SCORES

			TOTAL: MEDIAN STANDARD SCORE					
MEDIAN STANDARD SCORE	GRADE EQUIVALENT	AGE EQUIVALENT	MEDIAN STANDARD SCORE	GRADE EQUIVALENT	AGE EQUIVALENT	MEDIAN STANDARD SCORE	GRADE EQUIVALENT	AGE EQUIVALENT
104	2.0	6–3	132	4.8	9–9	160	8.2	13–6
105	2.1	6–4	133	4.9	9–10	161	8.3	13–9
106	2.2	6–6	134	5.0	10–0	162	8.5	14–0
107	2.3	6–7	135	5.1	10–1	163	8.7	14–4
108	2.4	6–9	136	5.2	10–3	164	8.8	14–10
109	2.5	6–10	137	5.3	10–4	165	9.0	15–4
110	2.6	7–0	138	5.4	10–5	166	9.2	16–0
111	2.7	7–1	139	5.5	10–7	167	9.4	16–8
112	2.8	7–3	140	5.6	10–8	168	9.6	17–4
113	2.9	7–4	141	5.7	10–10	169	9.8	18–2
•114	3.0	7–6	142	5.8	10–11	170	10.0	
115	3.1	7–7	143	6.0	11–1	171	10.3	
116	3.2	7–9	144	6.1	11–2	172	10.5	
117	3.3	7–10	145	6.2	11–4	173	10.8	
118	3.4	8–0	146	6.3	11–5	174	11.0	
119	3.5	8–1	147	6.4	11–7	175	11.3	
120	3.6	8–3	148	6.5	11–9	176	11.6	
121	3.7	8–4	149	6.7	11–10	177	11.9	
122	3.8	8–6	150	6.8	12–0	178	12.3	
123	3.9	8–7	151	6.9	12–1	179	12.7	
124	4.0	8–9	152	7.1	12–3	180	13.1	
125	4.1	8–10	153	7.2	12–5	181	13.6	
126	4.2	9–0	154	7.3	12–7	182	14.1	
127	4.3	9–1	155	7.5	12–8	183	14.8	
128	4.4	9–3	156	7.6	12–10	184	15.5	
129	4.5	9–4	157	7.7	13–0	185	16.3	
130	4.6	9–6	158	7.9	13–2			
131	4.7	9–7	159	8.0	13–4			

From Iowa Silent Reading Tests, Elementary Test, *Manual of Directions*. Reproduced by permission. Copyright 1933, 1939, 1943 by Harcourt, Brace & World, Inc., New York.

intervening scores are determined through interpolation. However, the same type of interpretation is valid for all scores. *A grade equivalent tells the grade placement of students for whom the given test performance is average.* For example, if a student had a median standard score of 138 on the Iowa silent reading test, it could be said that he is doing as well with the material covered by the test as the average students who are four-tenths of the way through the fifth grade.

One important caution should be taken in interpreting grade

equivalents. Remember always that they refer to typical performance with respect to the content covered by the test. If, for example, a second-grade student has a grade equivalent of 4.7 on a second-grade arithmetic test, this does not mean that he is master of the content of third- and fourth-grade arithmetic. This content is probably not covered by the second-grade arithmetic test. His score means that he does as well with the content of second-grade arithmetic as the average person who is seven tenths of the way through the fourth grade does *with this same content.*

It must also be remembered that grade equivalents are based on the *average* score for pupils at a given grade placement. Even if we have a class typical with respect to pupil mastery of the content covered by a test, we should not expect all students to have a grade equivalent equal to grade placement. Some will have grade equivalents above this and some below.

5. *Age equivalents* Another type of norm is the age equivalent. *The age equivalent expresses test performance in terms of age, in years and months, of persons for whom the given performance is the average.* In its method of development it is similar to the grade equivalent, except that the groups from which scores are derived are formed on the basis of equivalent ages rather than on identical grade placement.

Since Table 14 includes age as well as grade equivalents, we can refer to it to explain the former. The fact that the median standard score of 104 has an age equivalent of 6–3 tells us that the average score on this test for persons who were 6 years and 3 months in age was 104.

This type of score is not as widely used as are some of those discussed previously. Because pupils are exposed to subject content in terms of their grade placement rather than individual age, the expression of content mastery in terms of age equivalents is not too meaningful.

Reliability of the Test. Another type of data that must be obtained before a test is ready for final publication concerns its reliability, for which various procedures are used. An examination of test manuals will show that, of those techniques discussed in chapter six, the ones most commonly encountered are the split-halves, the alternate forms, and the Kuder-Richardson. Since each procedure provides slightly different information concerning the test, it is highly desirable that a manual present data on more than one type of reliability. Many test manuals do this.

As mentioned in the previous discussions of reliability, the alternate forms procedure, with a time lapse between the two testings, is generally the most rigorous procedure for determining reliability and, consequently, will yield the lowest reliability coefficients. Both the difference between forms and the instability associated with differences in time will tend to reduce the relationship between the two sets of scores. However, this type of reliability is most meaningful to the typical test user, for, if the score obtained from any test is to be considered a relatively true measure of the quality being assessed, it is important to know how independent it is of one particular sample of test items and of chance fluctuations produced merely by differences in time of administration. This information is provided by a coefficient of stability and equivalence.

A less rigorous estimate of reliability is obtained through the split-halves procedure in which two samples of test items are used, those in one half of the examination and those in the other, but in which there is no measure of stability over time. That is, since both halves are taken as parts of the same test, simultaneously, any physical or psychological conditions within students or any environmental influences on the examinees will be identical for both halves. Thus this method for determining reliability does not take into account the effect of any of these fluctuations that would be associated with differences in time. The split-halves reliability coefficient will be spuriously high if it is taken as estimating the same type of reliability as that provided by a coefficient of stability and equivalence. The Kuder-Richardson procedure, which is also based on only one administration of the test, has this same weakness in that it provides no indication of the stability of scores.

This discussion of factors affecting different types of reliability estimates should not be interpreted as suggesting the elimination of certain procedures, but merely as emphasizing the importance of a standardized test being accompanied by data on more than one type of reliability. If the student studies test manuals that provide such data, he will find that split-halves coefficients are generally slightly higher than coefficients for the same test determined through the alternate forms procedure.

The Test Manual.   One of the final steps in the production of a standardized test is the development of a manual or manuals which contain information on administering and scoring the test, plus data concerning its development, standardization, validity, and reliability. In some cases all the information is included in one booklet, while in others it appears in several booklets. These publications are given a variety of names such as "directions for administering and scoring," "technical manual," "directions for interpreting scores," and similar descriptive titles. Some idea as to the specific types of data found in such manuals can be obtained from many of the illustrations used in this chapter and in chapter six. The reader not already familiar with test manuals should secure a few samples of them to study.

If a test is to be used meaningfully the user should know not only how to administer and score it but also something about its validity and reliability and how it was developed and standardized. The manual is the first place to look for this information.

TYPES OF STANDARDIZED ACHIEVEMENT TEST

Anyone planning to use standardized achievement tests must recognize that there are different types of tests and test batteries. The following sections describe some of these.

General Achievement Batteries. Perhaps the most widely used type of achievement test is the achievement test battery made up of a number of subtests in a variety of areas. These batteries are available for all school levels from grades one through twelve and can be used to obtain a comprehensive picture of a student's attainment in the various areas of study. Such tests can best be understood through a brief survey of a few representative examples.

1. Iowa Tests of Basic Skills.[2] These may be used in grades three through eight and include eleven subtests: (1) vocabulary, (2) reading comprehension, (3) spelling, (4) capitalization, (5) punctuation, (6) language usage, (7) map reading, (8) reading graphs and tables, (9) knowledge and use of reference materials, (10) arithmetic concepts, and (11) arithmetic problem-solving. As its title suggests, the tests in this battery are concerned with the "basic skill" areas and do not attempt to measure a pupil's achievement in all subject-matter areas. Tests for all grade levels are contained in one test booklet, and items are arranged in order of level of difficulty. Each

2. Published by Houghton Mifflin Co., Boston.

grade starts and stops at different points in this sequence of items.

2. *Metropolitan Achievement Tests.*[3]   These tests are published in five different batteries: (1) Primary I, for grade 1 (four subtests); (2) Primary II, for grade 2 (five subtests); (3) Elementary, for grades 3 and 4 (eight subtests); (4) Intermediate, for grades 5 and 6 (twelve subtests); and (5) Advanced, for grades 7, 8, and 9 (thirteen subtests). As indicated, the number of subtests increases with grade level, reflecting the additional content areas to which a student is exposed as he advances through the grades. For example, the Primary I battery has tests in (1) word knowledge, (2) word discrimination, (3) reading, and (4) arithmetic concepts and skills, while the Advanced battery has tests in (1) word knowledge, (2) reading, (3) spelling, (4) arithmetic problem-solving and concepts, (5) computation, (6) language usage, (7) punctuation and capitalization, (8) parts of speech—grammar, (9) kinds of sentence, (10) language study skills, (11) social studies information, (12) social studies study skills, and (13) science.

3. *Sequential Tests of Educational Progress (STEP).*[4]   The STEP tests include seven different subtests, each in a separate test booklet, at the following levels: (1) Level 1, college freshmen and sophomores; (2) Level 2, grades 10, 11, and 12; (3) Level 3, grades 7, 8, and 9; and (4) Level 4, grades 4, 5, and 6. The manual for STEP states that these tests represent "a series growing out of the demands of educators for instruments measuring the broad outcomes of education, rather than the relatively narrow results of any specific subject-matter course." [5] The seven tests involved at each level are (1) reading, (2) writing, (3) listening, (4) essay, (5) social studies, (6) mathematics, and (7) science.

4. *Stanford Achievement Tests.*[6]   The latest edition of these tests, for grades 1 through 9, includes five different batteries: (1) Primary I, the middle of grade 1 to the middle of grade 2, with six tests in word reading, paragraph meaning, vocabulary, spelling, word study skills, and arithmetic; (2) Primary II, the middle of grade 2 to the end of grade 3, with eight tests in word meaning, paragraph meaning, science and social studies concepts, spelling,

---

3. Published by Harcourt, Brace & World, New York.
4. Published by Educational Testing Service, Princeton, N.J.
5. *STEP Manual for Interpreting Scores, Reading.* Copyright 1957 by Cooperative Test Division, Educational Testing Service, Princeton, N.J., p. 7.
6. Published by Harcourt, Brace & World, New York.

word study skills, language, arithmetic computation, and arithmetic concepts; (3) Intermediate I, the beginning of grade 4 to the middle of grade 5, with ten tests in word meaning, paragraph meaning, spelling, word study skills, language, arithmetic computation, arithmetic concepts, arithmetic applications, social studies, and science; (4) Intermediate II, the middle of grade 5 to the end of grade 6, with nine tests in word meaning, paragraph meaning, spelling, language, arithmetic computation, arithmetic concepts, arithmetic applications, social studies, and science; and (5) Advanced, the beginning of grade 7 to the end of grade 9, with eight tests in paragraph meaning, spelling, language, arithmetic computation, arithmetic concepts, arithmetic applications, social studies, and science. These batteries are published in single booklets. The Intermediate and Advanced batteries also appear in partial batteries which include all the tests except science and social studies. Some of the tests are also available individually.

This listing of tests is not intended to be at all comprehensive nor to suggest that those described are superior to others available. It merely illustrates the composition of some typical achievement batteries. Descriptions of many other tests of this type will be found in the catalogues of major test publishers as well as in *The Sixth Mental Measurements Yearbook.*[7]

Achievement batteries differ both in the grades covered and in the nature of their subtests. Persons selecting such tests will have to take into consideration the rationale underlying the test as well as its specific content. General achievement batteries are useful in providing an overall survey of pupil attainment and are helpful in comparing an individual student's relative standing in different areas. It can be diagnostic to the extent of identifying specific subjects or skills in which he may be weak. This type of diagnosis may also be useful in investigating the strengths and weaknesses of an entire class or of a total school program, or in other situations where it is useful to have measures that permit comparisons of relative achievement in different content or skill areas.

Tests in Specific Content Areas. For many purposes it is helpful to have a standardized achievement test that confines itself to one content area. A teacher of a given subject such as chemistry, algebra,

---

7. Oscar K. Buros, ed. (Highland Park, N.J.: Gryphon Press, 1965).

or geometry may be interested only in how well his students are doing in that subject. To employ an entire battery would be wasteful. Furthermore, because no battery is so comprehensive as to include all subjects, many teachers at the junior and senior high levels find that their subjects are not covered by the batteries used in their schools. Also, in a comprehensive achievement battery, no subtest can be long enough to afford much basis for diagnosis of strengths and weaknesses within any one subject. These are some of the reasons teachers wish to have tests that are limited to one subject.

If one consults the standard sources for the listings of published tests, he will find that there are a great number available in most subject-matter areas. Since they are so numerous and since they differ greatly in the extent and manner in which they provide for subscores within an area, it would be of little use to list available tests or give examples. The only way a teacher can become familiar with what is available in a given area is to consult such sources as the Mental Measurements yearbooks [8] and then make a detailed analysis of the content and technical quality of available tests by actually securing copies of them.

USING A STANDARDIZED ACHIEVEMENT TEST

Preceding sections of this chapter have necessarily contained many suggestions and implications for the selection and use of standardized achievement tests. However, additional important suggestions should be made, and certain points re-emphasized.

Selecting a Test. A first step in selecting a test is to determine exactly what purpose it is intended to serve. One should consider how the scores are to be used as well as the content and abilities to be tested.

A second basic step is to become aware of the tests that are available in the area of concern. Major help on this step can be obtained by consulting recent editions of the Mental Measurements yearbooks.[9] These yearbooks include descriptions and reviews of essentially all published tests of achievement, aptitude, interest, person-

---

8. *Ibid.*, and Oscar K. Buros, ed., *The Fifth Mental Measurements Yearbook* (Highland Park, N.J.: Gryphon Press, 1961).
9. *Ibid.*

ality, and other qualities. In addition to a detailed description of the test, each yearbook presents a critical review by at least one expert in the given area. While such reviews must be looked upon as presenting the judgment of that one person, they are helpful as a starting point for the assessment of any test. Also of help in this step are the catalogues put out by the various test publishing agencies.

Test catalogues and the reviews provided in the Buros volumes will aid in identifying those tests that should be given careful consideration for use in a particular situation. When these tests have been identified, copies of each, together with manuals and other related materials, should be secured. Next, each test should be studied, item by item, to see if it has the desired *content validity*. The manual should be given a careful scrutiny to determine the *reliability* and the procedures used in the *standardization* of the instrument. Consideration should also be given to whether the *types of norm* provided will be the most useful ones. Another important consideration is the *time required for administering* the test. Does the latter make it feasible to use the test in the given circumstances? Less important criteria include the probable *ease of administration, ease of scoring,* and *cost*. When several tests are being considered for a given purpose, they can be compared and judged as to their relative standings on each of the above characteristics. The potential test user should also employ the standards implied in the discussions of the criteria in preceding sections of this book.

Using Standardized Achievement Tests. In describing various types of standardized achievement tests and their development, we have touched on some of the purposes of these instruments. These purposes, plus additional uses, can be summarized as follows:

1. Scores from standardized tests provide an outside criterion, independent of teacher judgment, that can be useful in several ways. The teacher can compare his class with classes in a large, representative group of schools; and, although test norms must never be used as standards, the teacher who takes into account the aptitude of his pupils can use the norms to make judgments about his class's achievement. The norms provide a much broader basis for judgments of the relative attainment of individual pupils than that provided by comparisons within the class. The fact that the

test has not been developed by the teacher should cause the pupil, his parents, and others to accept the score as an impartial assessment, not merely a biased judgment of the teacher.

2. Because many achievement tests, particularly the comprehensive batteries, provide successive grade-level forms that can be given each year, it is possible to examine rates of pupil growth in yearly spans. This is difficult, if not impossible, to do with the scores obtained from teacher-made tests.

3. In the achievement batteries in which scores on all subtests are based on the same standardization samples, it is possible to make comparisons of relative achievement in different subjects both for individual students and for a total class. This permits a certain amount of diagnosis of strengths and weaknesses.

4. Scores from standardized tests are particularly useful when students transfer from one school district to another. Because the meaning of teacher-assigned grades differs markedly from school to school, scores from published tests may be essential in making decisions concerning placement of transfer students.

5. Scores from standardized achievement tests have been found to be useful predictors of future academic success. Their comprehensiveness and reliability have led to their use, particularly at the secondary school level, as important supplements to grade-point average and aptitude test scores in predicting achievement in college or some other type of later schooling.

Uses to Be Avoided.   In some instances, results from standardized achievement tests are used in ways not intended by the test producer nor warranted by the type of information they provide. Here are some of the uses that should be avoided.

1. Test norms should not be used as standards that determine the level of satisfactory achievement. For example, if a test is given to a class that is midway through the third grade, a grade equivalent of 3.5 should not automatically be considered as defining the level these students should achieve. This score does represent the achievement on this test for typical pupils who are halfway through grade three, but the chances are that any single class is not really "typical." If pupils in this hypothetical class are above average in intelligence or scholastic aptitude, then one probably would expect them to do better than 3.5. Of course, the reverse would be true if they are below average in aptitude. One must always remember

that norms are based on performances of typical or average students and cannot be considered as defining the standards that all classes or students should attain.

2. Scores from standardized achievement tests should not be used as the basis for assigning pupil grades. Tests and other evaluation devices that have been developed by the teacher and used regularly throughout the term generally provide a much more comprehensive and valid assessment of overall pupil achievement. Results from such procedures should provide the major basis for determining a pupil's grade.

3. Test results cannot be used to judge the effectiveness of teaching. The factors that affect pupil learning are so numerous and their interaction so complex that to attempt to ascribe the amount of learning that takes place within a class to any one factor (such as teacher performance) is entirely unrealistic. Also, standardized tests measure only certain types of academic achievement and are not intended to provide a complete assessment of all that a pupil has gained as a result of being in a classroom. Perhaps the most important reason for not using pupil test scores to evaluate teachers is that, where this has been tried, the inevitable result has been that teachers lose sight of the broad variety of goals toward which they should be guiding their pupils and merely "teach for the test."

Administering the Test. A rather common point of discussion concerning the use of standardized achievement tests is whether such tests should be given at the beginning or at the end of the school year. Actually, in view of the many different types of tests that are available and the variety of purposes for which they can be used, a test could be used at almost any time during the school year. The information that different tests provide will be useful at different times, depending on the use to which it is to be put. Decisions as to when particular tests are to be administered should be made on the basis of the overall plan for testing and evaluation.

Strong arguments can be presented for giving comprehensive achievement test batteries near the beginning of the school year rather than in the spring, as is done rather conventionally. The basic use for such test results should be as aids in the improvement of instruction, and tests given at the start of the year provide up-to-date information on all students enrolled for that term. These data would seem to be essential for planning instructional programs for individual pupils as well as for the total class. There is general agreement that standardized test scores should not be used to grade pupils or to evaluate the effectiveness of a teacher, and giving such tests at the start of the year reduces the likelihood of their being used in these ways. These reasons suggest that, in planning the time for the administration of tests, some thought should be given to how the results should *not* be used as well as to how they are to be used.

An essential part of the meaning of the term "standardized test" is that such a test is to be administered under carefully specified standard conditions. If the norms are to have a true meaning for any given situation, the test must be given according to the procedures used with the norm sample, those prescribed in the test manual. The instructions to the student must be read exactly as specified, time limits must be rigidly followed, and other conditions must be arranged as stipulated in the directions. Fortunately, the manuals for most tests contain clear and complete specifications. These should be followed exactly; the teacher must resist any temptation to depart from them.

SUMMARY

Standardized achievement tests can be important tools for the professional teacher who knows how to select and use such instruments. In general, these tests have been produced by experienced personnel, meet rather high standards with respect to the technical qualities of a good test, and have an established degree of reliability. The norms that accompany them permit a comparison of the achievement of students in any local school or classroom with that of a large group of rather typical students at the same school level. Such scores also provide a basis for diagnosis of pupil strengths and weaknesses, for the study of yearly growth, and for many other comparisons that are not possible with the results of teacher-made tests. While the educator recognizes these many important uses of standardized test results, he should also be alert to avoid some of the common misuses, such as employing the norms as standards or using the scores to grade pupils or to assess teacher effectiveness. The teacher who is aware of how published tests are developed, who is acquainted with the criteria that should be used in the evaluation of such instruments, and who knows the sources to use in investigating available tests should be able to locate standardized achievement tests that will be of major assistance in providing important information concerning students.

Suggestions for Class Discussion and Further Investigation

1. Secure copies of tests and test manuals for several standardized achievement tests. Study each manual to determine what each publisher feels a given test is designed to measure and then study the test itself to determine how well it covers what it is intended to measure. Compare your judgments with those of your classmates.
2. For each test investigated in Suggestion 1, note also such things as the composition of the standardization group, the size of the reported reliability coefficients, and the method used to determine reliability. Rank the tests with respect to their adequacy on each of these points. Discuss your rankings with your classmates.
3. Consult the Mental Measurements yearbooks (fifth and sixth) and note what the reviewers say about each of the tests you examined in Suggestions 1 and 2. Do you agree with the assessments of the reviewers?
4. The use of standardized tests is sometimes criticized on the basis that it may tend to dictate what is taught in a school. Under what conditions might this happen? How might this be avoided even though standardized tests were used? Are there any conditions under which some degree of "dictation" of this type might be helpful?
5. Assume that you are responsible for developing a testing program for kindergarten through twelfth grade in a given school system. Outline what you would consider to be the most desirable testing program and show exactly when and where you would use specific types of achievement test.

Suggestions for Further Reading

An essential type of reading to supplement this chapter is of a variety of published achievement tests and their accompanying manuals. Tests catalogues and the tests themselves can be obtained from such major test publishers as:

1. California Test Bureau, Del Monte Research Park, Monterey, California 93940
2. Educational Test Bureau, Division of American Guidance Service, Inc., 720 Washington Avenue S.E., Minneapolis, Minnesota 55414
3. Educational Testing Service, Cooperative Test Division, Princeton, New Jersey 08541
4. Harcourt, Brace & World, Inc., Test Department, 757 Third Avenue, New York, New York 10017
5. Houghton Mifflin Company, 110 Tremont Street, Boston, Massachusetts 02107
6. The Psychological Corporation, 304 East 45th Street, New York, New York 10017
7. Science Research Associates, Inc., 259 East Erie Street, Chicago, Illinois 60611

Extensive reading should also be done in the Mental Measurements yearbooks, discussed briefly in the chapter, edited by Oscar K. Buros, *The Sixth Mental Measurements Yearbook* (Highland Park, N.J.; Gryphon Press, 1965); and *The Fifth Mental Measurements Yearbook* (1961).

Good discussions of standardized achievement tests and of their uses will be found in: Lee J. Cronbach, *Essentials of Psychological Testing,* 2nd ed. (New York: Harper & Row, 1960), ch. 13; Norman E. Gronlund, *Measurement and Evaluation in Teaching* (New York: Macmillan, 1965), chs. 12–14; Robert L. Thorndike and Elizabeth Hagen, *Measurement and Evaluation in Psychology and Education* (New York: Wiley, 1955), ch. 11.

Chapter Eight

Tests of Scholastic Aptitude

There are many occasions when it is important that the teacher or other educator be able to predict the chances of a student's future success in the classroom or in some line of work. A first-grade teacher needs to know when a pupil is ready to profit from formal instruction in beginning reading. A junior high school homeroom teacher may be called upon to consult with a pupil concerning his chances of success in high school algebra. A high school guidance counselor must frequently advise students on the probability of their success in college or in some other type of post–high school study. In these and similar situations educators use information from a variety of sources to estimate pupil aptitude.

It is generally recognized that the best predictor of a student's success in any type of course work is the record of his achievement in that or a related type of study. The best indicator of success in college is the high school scholastic record. The scores that a student makes on mathematics achievement tests covering his seventh and eighth grade work are a good predictor of success in high school algebra; since the same factors that have influenced past performance are likely to be the major determiners of future achievement, it is not surprising that teachers are primarily dependent on past school records to determine the aptitude of students for almost any type of school work.

However, there are occasions when supplementary evidence is essential. The teacher who wants to determine the scholastic aptitude of a beginning first-grade student has no records upon which to base this judgment. Also, at any grade level, the records of many students present conflicting evidence as to their aptitudes for a

particular type of study. A student's progress in a given field may
show a rather uneven trend marked by success at one time followed by relative failure. The teacher, then, is concerned with the
real aptitude of a particular student for a certain type of work.
Also, the meaning of past academic record in the form of grades
varies greatly from school to school, causing confusion when students transfer from one school to another or when they move from
high school to college. Such reasons have made standard tests of
scholastic aptitude important tools for teachers and school officials.

The person who has made no previous study of tests of this type
or of the general theory of testing in this area must realize that
aptitude and intelligence tests are not designed to measure some
type of innate capacity entirely independent of previous experience
or schooling. A person's intelligence or mental ability, as measured
by testing devices, depends to a great extent on his environment,
the influences of people around him, and his experiences. Tests of
scholastic aptitude, including the so-called tests of readiness, of
intelligence, and of general mental ability, as well as those tests
that include the word *aptitude* in their titles, measure aptitude
indirectly by measuring what the pupil has actually learned. This
method of testing is based on the common sense assumption that
the only way in which aptitude can be measured is by determining
the extent to which a student has actually applied that aptitude in
acquiring a certain amount of knowledge by a given stage in his
career. As a result, many of the items found on aptitude tests
resemble the items found on achievement tests.

The essential difference between achievement tests and aptitude
tests is that an achievement test measures abilities a student is to
have acquired as a result of some specific amount of instruction he
has received in a given instructional sequence, while an aptitude
test measures what a pupil has learned as a result of some more
general experience and is not centered on the specific objectives
of instruction for a particular course. For example, an achievement
test given at the end of the first grade or at the start of the second
grade would be based on subject-matter content that the pupil had
studied during his first year in school, but the items found on an
intelligence or an aptitude test given at that same time would be
based on material that the typical child of that age would have
been expected to learn as a result of everyday experience.

Because of these differences between achievement and aptitude tests, predictions as to future scholastic success made on the basis of these two types of instrument will differ significantly for a few students. Occasionally a student who has considerable aptitude for a particular course may show rather poor achievement when tested because he has not applied himself to his study. This student may show a much higher score on the aptitude test than on the achievement test, and, if his study habits can be changed before he starts work on a succeeding course or unit of study, his aptitude test score may be more predictive of the actual success he will have in that course than would his previous achievement as evidenced by his achievement test score. On the other hand, if his study habits do not change and he fails to apply himself with greater ambition to study the future course, his aptitude test score would be misleading as an indicator of how well he should be expected to do. Aptitude test scores should not be looked upon as a measure of some innate capacity or some measure of absolute potential of a student, but rather as information supplementary to past academic record and to achievement test scores as an indicator of a student's chances for success in some specific type of future academic work.

The aptitude tests that are used in schools may be placed in four major categories: (1) general scholastic aptitude or intelligence tests, (2) readiness tests, (3) aptitude test batteries, and (4) tests for measuring aptitude for some one subject. Since general scholastic aptitude or intelligence tests are by far the most frequently used of the four types, our discussion of aptitude tests will begin with a consideration of them.

GENERAL SCHOLASTIC APTITUDE OR INTELLIGENCE TESTS

Since present-day intelligence tests are very much a product of the historical development of testing in this area, it is essential that the person who uses such tests have a general understanding of the history of intelligence testing. This history can be considered as beginning with the work of Alfred Binet, the French physician and psychologist who was active in the late nineteenth and early twentieth centuries in the study of mental traits. During the early part of his career, Binet was interested in studying and identifying factors that might be predictive of a person's ability to carry out simple tasks. Among the variables he tested in seeking a predictor of this type were such things as the size of a person's head and the amount of food that he consumes in a given period of time. Early in the 1900's, because of his interest in this problem, the Paris school system selected Binet as a member of a committee which was to develop a procedure for identifying children who could be expected to profit from instruction in the first grade. In other words, their job was to develop some type of measure of general scholastic aptitude.

The result of the committee's work was the scale published in 1905 by Alfred Binet and Theodore Simon. This first scale consisted of thirty different simple tasks or tests arranged in order of increasing difficulty. Experiments with this first scale on normal and subnormal children enabled Binet to determine a point on the scale that divided the students who could profit from normal classroom instruction from those who probably would not be able to succeed in the average classroom.

In 1908, Binet revised his earlier scale to include fifty-nine tasks and assigned each task to an age level (ages three to thirteen), thus introducing the concept of "mental age." The tests on these scales were administered individually by an examiner. Examples of the tasks on Binet's scale would include asking the examinee to point to the different parts of his body, repeat a certain number of digits, count coins, repeat a sentence, name colors, define words, and use words in a sentence.

The Binet-Simon scale seemed to show great promise and attracted considerable attention in several other countries. Although several persons worked on translations and adaptations of the Binet scale for use in this country, by far the most successful of these was the work of Lewis M. Terman of Stanford University. Terman's first Stanford revision of the Binet scale appeared in 1916 and was followed by revisions in 1937 and 1960.

The person administering the Stanford-Binet test must be given special training typically offered in a graduate course in psychology. In using the test he first attempts to determine the examinee's "basal age," the highest age level at which he can pass all six tests. With the average student the examiner will probably start testing at the age level one year below the examinee's chronological age. If the student cannot pass all tasks at this level, the examiner then works downward through the age levels until he finds the age at which the student can pass all tasks. The tester works upward from the student's basal age in administering all tests at age levels above that, recording the number of tests successfully answered by the student at each age level, until an upper level is reached at which the examinee can answer none of the tasks correctly. When this level is reached, the examining stops. A basic type of score in intelligence or general scholastic aptitude testing is the *mental age*. On the Stanford-Binet test, mental age is determined by adding to a student's basal age two months of credit for every task that he passes above the level of his basal age. What this involves can be illustrated by the following hypothetical results:

Subject's performance	Credit received
Passes all tests at year 10	10 years (basal age)
Passes 3 of 6 tests at year 11	6 months
Passes 2 of 6 tests at year 12	4 months
Passes no test at year 13 (testing stops)	
	MA = 10 years 10 months

The student in the above example has an actual age of 9 years 1 month. Since he passed all items at year 8, he took the following tests until, at year 13, he passed none of the items. He was given a mental age (MA) of 10 years 10 months, receiving 2 months credit for each item above year 10 (basal age) answered correctly.

A second basic type of score that is obtained from an intelligence test is the intelligence quotient or IQ. This score provides an indication of the relative "brightness" of a student, in comparison with his age, and can be computed from the following formula:

$$IQ = \frac{MA}{CA} \times 100$$

In the above situation, the student, who has a chronological age (CA) of 9 years 1 month, will have an IQ of 119. The ages are converted into months:

$$IQ = \frac{10 \text{ years } 10 \text{ months}}{9 \text{ years } 1 \text{ month}} \times 100 = \frac{130}{109} \times \frac{100}{1} = 119$$

Although the determination of IQ, as in the earlier editions of the Stanford-Binet, by the ratio of a child's mental age to his chronological age is not used in figuring IQ's from many intelligence tests, including the 1960 edition of the Stanford-Binet, the ratio is a useful definition of IQ. From this formula it can be seen that the IQ is a measure of relative aptitude that takes the child's age into account and permits a comparison of aptitude among persons of differing ages. If the mental age is equivalent to the actual age, the ratio of the two multiplied by 100, or the IQ, is 100. The average IQ, then, is about 100. However, by the time students reach high school, some of the less capable have dropped out. College is a further selective agent, choosing only the better students. Therefore, the average IQ of high school or college students will be higher than 100.

An examiner must have extensive training and practice before he is prepared to administer individual intelligence tests such as the Stanford-Binet. One cannot expect to become prepared for this merely by taking a general course in testing. Hence, the present discussion of individual tests is not intended to be complete but is merely a brief introduction to one test, the Stanford-Binet. One reason for providing this introduction is that the Stanford-Binet is widely used, and many teachers will have access to results from this test where the actual testing has been done by a school psychologist or other trained person.[1] Perhaps the more important reason, however, is that since the Stanford-Binet was the first widely used test of intelligence and since it has maintained its position as somewhat the standard measure of intelligence for so many years, one can understand other tests only to the extent that he can relate them to the Stanford-Binet. Many tests are descendents of this scale in the sense that they attempt to measure the same thing. Test manuals often discuss the similarity of a given test to the Binet and in many cases present correlations between scores from the two tests. In some other cases a test manual may describe how that test is different from the Binet. In either case it is used as a point of reference.

Group Tests of Intelligence. Since the Stanford-Binet was developed at a time when published group tests of achievement were starting to receive considerable attention, it was natural that consideration was given at that early stage to the development of intelligence tests that could be administered to groups in the same way

---

1. Other widely used individual tests are the *Wechsler Intelligence Scale for Children,* WISC, and the *Wechsler Adult Intelligence Scale,* WAIS, both published by The Psychological Corporation, New York.

that achievement tests were administered. The work of many persons who were concerned with such development was brought to a head during World War I when a number of them collaborated to produce a test that could be used to obtain a quick measure of the aptitude of men in the armed forces. The result was the Army Alpha, the first widely used group intelligence test. After this breakthrough, the years immediately following the war saw the development of a number of these paper-and-pencil tests, and their popularity has resulted in the continuing development of such instruments in the years since then. Group tests can be given much more economically, in terms of both time and money, than can individual tests; they can be administered by the typical classroom teacher; and they have been shown to produce essentially the same results as do individual tests, so it is not surprising that they have come to be the most widely used measures of intelligence.

Types of Group Test. The *omnibus* test is perhaps the most common of the scholastic aptitude or intelligence tests. It does not measure separate aspects of aptitude, but combines into one test items that seem to be measuring abilities of a number of different types. This procedure is a continuation of the precedent of the Stanford-Binet test, which also combines performance on a variety of tasks to yield one general measure of mental ability. An example of a group test of the omnibus type is the Otis Quick-scoring Mental Ability Test. Figure 25 gives some idea of the variety of items found on this test—figure relations, information, arithmetic reasoning, general reasoning, mixed sentences, classification, word meaning, and number series. On a logical basis it would appear that some of these items should be most highly related to achievement in verbal types of learning, others to numerical, and others to learning involving figures. However, an omnibus test does not involve the separation of items on such a basis. Instead it is built on the assumption that combining items that measure a variety of abilities so as to produce one test score will provide a broad and reliable measure of a pupil's general aptitude for school work. Items on such a test need not correlate highly with one another. The only requirement is that performance on the items be correlated with the increase in ability that is associated with increase in age.

While most omnibus tests provide only one score, that is, one

30 Three of the four designs at the right are alike in some way. Which one is not like the other three?

(51)   (52)   (53)   (54)

31 Which of the sentences below tells best what a puppy is?
(56) **It barks and has fur.** (57) **It is a playful animal.** (58) **It is a small animal with four legs.**
(59) **It barks and has fur.** (60) **It is a young dog.** ....

32 If oranges are 6 for a quarter, how much will two dozen oranges cost?
(61) 24¢   (62) 60¢   (63) 72¢   (64) $1.00   (65) $1.50 ....

33 If Helen is younger than Grace and Helen is younger than Alice, then Alice is (?) Grace.
(66) younger than   (67) older than   (68) the same age as   (69) *cannot say which*

34 If the following words were rearranged to make the best sentence, with what letter would the *last* word of the sentence begin?
twigs **a** *gathers* *bird* *nest* *its* *for*
(71) **t**   (72) **g**   (73) **b**   (74) **n**   (75) **f** ....

35 Which of the five things below is most like a violin, a flute, and a cornet?
(76) **a radio**   (77) **a saxophone**   (78) **a phonograph**   (79) **a drum**   (80) **music** ....

36 The carbon copy of a letter is said to be —
(81) **a carbonate**   (82) **a counterfeit**   (83) **a duplicate**   (84) **an imitation**   (85) **a multiple**

37 Which of the following is most like an orange, a banana, and a prune?
(1) **a tree**   (2) **a peach**   (3) **a peel**   (4) **a nut**   (5) **food** ....

38 Which of the five words below does not belong with the others?
(6) **tall**   (7) **honest**   (8) **strong**   (9) **healthy**   (10) **handsome** ....

39 One number is wrong in the following series.   What should that number be?
8 1 7 1 6 1 5 1 4 1 3 1 2 1 0 1
(11) **2**   (12) **3**   (13) **1**   (14) **4**   (15) **5** ....

general mental age and IQ, some tests of this type provide two scores, *verbal* and *nonverbal* (language and nonlanguage), and items are placed in one of the two subtests on the basis of whether they involve the use of words or the use of figures and numbers only. In some cases such separate scores can provide interesting and useful information. They may help to identify the student whose lack of verbal facility is making him appear to have less mental ability than he actually has. One score may provide a check on the other. However, verbal and nonverbal scores are usually quite highly correlated, and for many students there is little difference between the two measures. It should also be recognized that nonverbal or nonlanguage tests are not actually independent of the student's verbal ability. Because the directions in almost all cases are given through the printed or spoken word, the student who has a weakness in verbal comprehension will be handicapped even on the nonverbal test. When verbal and nonverbal scores are compared as to their predictive validity for school subjects, the nonverbal scores are generally found to have somewhat lower correlations for most types of schoolwork. This is to be expected since most subjects are verbally oriented.

In contrast with the omnibus type of group intelligence test, a few tests do group items measuring the same ability into a subtest and provide for several scores of separate mental abilities through the use of such subtests. These are generally referred to as *factor-type tests*, because a basic procedure in determining which subtests should be used is a mathematical one known as factor analysis. Factor analysis is initiated by determining the intercorrelations among a large number of different subtests of mental ability. By examining such correlation coefficients it is possible to determine which abilities seem to be closely related and which are quite independent. The mathematics involved in factor analysis is quite complex, but the typical test user will understand factor analysis sufficiently if he realizes that it is a procedure for identifying certain relatively independent dimensions in a given area of interest. Persons interested in intelligence testing have used it to identify

---

FIGURE 25

Otis Quick-Scoring Mental Ability Tests, New Edition, Beta FM. Reproduced by permission. Copyright 1954 by Harcourt, Brace & World, Inc., New York.

what they consider to be certain basic dimensions or factors in the measurement of intelligence.

Perhaps the best known test of the factor type is the SRA Primary Mental Abilities Test, produced by L. L. and Thelma Gwinn Thurstone, two pioneers in this type of test development. This instrument has subtests for five factors or abilities: (1) verbal-meaning, (2) space, (3) reasoning, (4) number, and (5) word-fluency. Each of the subtests supposedly measures a somewhat different type of aptitude, and it is hypothesized that each will be most valid for predicting performance in certain defined types of educational or occupational performance. That is, verbal-meaning scores should be most useful in predicting achievement in English and foreign language courses, while the space score should be most valid for such courses as geometry, mechanical drawing, and art.

Actually the results from the use of factor-type test scores have been quite mixed. In some cases they have been found to be quite useful, while in other instances measures of general intelligence have proven to be as valid for prediction of performance in most school subjects. Whether a factor score will be a better predictor for a given subject depends on the individual situation.

Using Intelligence Test Results.   Intelligence test scores are easily misinterpreted and sometimes misused. They are not pure measures of innate ability or latent capacity. The foregoing discussion should have made it clear that intelligence tests are measures of what a person can do. They determine a person's capacity by measuring how he has used that capacity to learn certain things. The test items call for the student to display knowledge or abilities that the typical person has had the opportunity to acquire. As a result, performance on the test will depend on the environment in which the person has been raised and the experiences that he has had. Someone who has been raised in an impoverished environment or in an environment that differs to any extent from that of the typical child will be handicapped as far as his performance on the test is concerned. For example, it has been shown that children from slum areas of large cities, from isolated Indian reservations, and from families where a foreign language is the usual means of communication have higher abilities than their scores on intelligence tests would indicate. It might be said that the tests discriminate against such persons. However, to the extent that instruction is based on the assumption that children come to school with certain common background experiences that have a bearing on intelligence test performance, it would be more correct to say that society or the schools discriminate against such culturally different pupils. Efforts have been made to develop "culture-free" or "culture-fair" tests, but they have not been used very widely.

It should also be re-emphasized that intelligence tests are intended to measure aptitude for typical schoolwork. Scores do not indicate aptitude for artistic tasks, creativity, social adaptability, or any of a great number of other abilities. They are measures of a limited type of aptitude—that required for performance in academic-type tasks. However, information on this type of aptitude can be very useful to the teacher if it is recognized for what it is and used properly.

The Meaning of Intelligence Test Scores. We have seen that intelligence test results are typically reported as mental ages (MA) and intelligence quotients (IQ). The teacher will find uses for both types of score. A mental age, of course, tells the chronological ages of persons for whom this level of aptitude is typical. It reveals something about the level of ability of a student and is particularly useful where it is known that a given level of aptitude is usually necessary if a student is to profit from a certain type of instruction. For example, some schools set a minimum mental age as a criterion for admission to first grade. Some reading programs suggest that a child should have attained an MA of at least six years before he starts formal instruction in reading.

The student's aptitude *relative* to that of other students his own age is evidenced by his IQ. We have already seen that a person's IQ may be defined as the ratio, multiplied by 100, of mental age to chronological age. This means that the person who is above average in intelligence will have an IQ above 100, while the person who is below average will have an IQ of less than 100. As with most types of scores, the IQ takes on real meaning only when we know something about the distribution of such measures for a representative group of persons. A commonly used reference group for this type of general discussion of the meaning of IQ's of various sizes is the standardization group for the 1937 revision of the Stanford-Binet test. This distribution is presented in Table 15. Note that the IQ's are somewhat normally distributed about a

TABLE 15

DISTRIBUTION OF IQ'S FOR THE STANDARDIZATION GROUP
FOR THE 1937 REVISION OF THE STANFORD-BINET TEST
(MEAN = 101.8, STANDARD DEVIATION = 16.4) *

IQ	Percent	Classification
160–69	0.03	
150–59	0.2	Very superior
140–49	1.1	
130–39	3.1	Superior
120–29	8.2	
110–19	18.1	High average
100–09	23.5	Normal or average
90–99	23.0	
80–89	14.5	Low average
70–79	5.6	Borderline defective
60–69	2.0	
50–59	0.4	Mentally defective
40–49	0.2	
30–39	0.03	

* Lewis M. Terman and Maud A. Merrill, *Stanford-Binet Intelligence Scale* (Boston: Houghton Mifflin Co., 1960), p. 18.

mean slightly above 100 and that the standard deviation is 16.4. A use of the percentages at each IQ level can provide a means for determining the relative superiority or inferiority of any given measure. Although different tests will differ slightly in the distribution of IQ's that they yield, one will not be in error to any great extent if he thinks of the general distribution of IQ's as being close to that presented in this table. Of course it must be recognized that the data in Table 15 are based on a sample representing the total range in ability running from mentally defective to genius. Samples taken from students attending school do not include persons with IQ's in the lower categories, and this trend is greater with the increase in school grade as the slower students are retained or are removed from regular school programs.

Some idea of the relationship of progress in school to distribution of IQ can be gained by reference to Table 16, which is based on data in the *Handbook* for the *Kuhlmann-Anderson Intelligence Tests*. This table shows the distribution of IQ's for pupils who are "on-grade," for those who are "retarded" (a year or more older

TABLE 16

DISTRIBUTION OF IQ'S FOR RETARDED, ON-GRADE,
AND ACCELERATED PUPILS IN GRADES 1–8
FOR KUHLMANN-ANDERSON INTELLIGENCE TEST *

IQ	Retarded group	On-grade group	Accelerated group	Total group
150+	—	—	1	1
145	—	—	1	1
140	—	1	4	5
135	—	1	8	9
130	—	—	23	23
125	—	9	30	39
120	—	23	102	125
115	—	42	145	187
110	2	108	263	373
105	4	211	337	552
100	9	320	311	640
95	26	275	185	486
90	64	209	109	382
85	102	119	34	255
80	109	71	15	195
75	84	25	6	115
70	61	5	4	70
65	41	2	—	43
60	19	—	—	19
55	3	—	—	3
50	5	—	—	5
N =	529	1,421	1,578	3,528

* F. Kuhlmann and Rose G. Anderson, *Handbook, Kuhlmann-Anderson Intelligence Tests* (Princeton, N.J.: Personnel Press, 1952), p. 13.

than typical students of their grade), and for those who are "accelerated" (a year or more younger than typical students of their grade). At least two important points are emphasized by the data in Table 16. They show that the average IQ is higher as one goes from the retarded students to the on-grade students to the accelerated students, but that there is a considerable overlapping of IQ's among the groups. That is, not all accelerated students have high IQ's, nor do all retarded students have low IQ's. The correlation between IQ and academic achievement is far from perfect. A second point brought out by this table is that a teacher must expect the average IQ for any given group of students to deviate from 100 to the extent that the group is not truly representative of the overall student population. The person teaching in a school in a culturally deprived area might anticipate having students whose distribution of intelligence quotients would approach that for the retarded group shown in the first column of Table 16. On the other hand, the teacher working in a neighborhood having a high socioeconomic level might be dealing with students more nearly represented by the distribution for the accelerated group.

The Stability of the IQ. An interesting question in using the intelligence quotient is the extent to which a person's IQ will remain constant over the years. There is some definite tendency toward constancy; that is, most persons maintain a somewhat stable level of relative aptitude for schoolwork throughout their school careers. This, however, does not mean that we can expect a person's IQ to be exactly the same from one testing to the next. Several factors influence the stability of the IQ.

1. Even if a subject's "true" intelligence quotient did remain constant from one testing to the next, there would be some variation in measured IQ due merely to the less-than-perfect reliability of the test. Such variability can easily be as large as five or ten IQ units.

2. If IQ's are obtained at two testings through the use of two different tests, we can expect some variation due to the difference in tests. In one study of this problem Roger T. Lennon [2] determined equivalent IQ's for three different tests, the Terman-McNemar Test of Mental Ability, the Otis Quick-scoring Mental Ability Gamma Test, and the Pintner General Ability Verbal Series Advanced Test. Some representative equivalent IQ's selected at different points along the IQ scale are shown below. This table shows, for example, that a person with an IQ of 141 as measured

Terman IQ	Otis IQ	Pintner IQ
141	134	138
120	116	118
102	100	99
80	83	74
66	76	64

2. *Test Service Notebook Number 11* (New York: Harcourt, Brace & World, 1952).

by the Terman-McNemar test would be expected to have an IQ of 134 on the Otis and 138 on the Pintner. Other studies have shown that these types of difference among tests are rather typical. If the IQ of a given student is measured on two occasions by a different instrument at each testing, there may well be some difference in the scores that could be accounted for solely by the differences in the tests.

3. A third source of instability in intelligence quotients is actual change in the student. Previous sections have emphasized that performance on intelligence tests is affected by the background of the student and the type of experience he has had. A student who comes from a home life and general environment quite different from that of the typical family could be expected to be handicapped in taking an intelligence test when he first enters school. If, during the ensuing years, however, his home environment changes, or if the school environment is such as to enrich his general background, his measured intelligence will probably increase. That is, with some students there will be significant changes in measured IQ produced by fundamental changes in the culture to which the student is exposed.

In summary, a person's IQ may vary by as much as five or ten or even fifteen points from one testing to the next solely on the basis of the unreliability of the scores or changes in the test being used. Variations of this size, then, probably do not indicate any change in actual aptitude, and for the majority of persons changes over time will be only of a magnitude that can be attributed to unreliability. However, for some persons significant changes in the experiences to which they are exposed or in their physical or mental health may produce much larger shifts in measured aptitude.

Validity of Intelligence Tests. Manuals for intelligence tests typically provide data on the predictive and concurrent validities of the test. Evidence on concurrent validity indicates how close a given test comes to measuring the same thing as some other intelligence test or how closely scores are related to performance on some measure of achievement. Since intelligence test scores are used most frequently for predicting some type of achievement, the most important evidence on validity is that concerning predictive validity. The test manual will probably provide some information showing how well the intelligence test results correlate with later measures of achievement such as test scores or course grades. Examples of data of this type were presented and discussed in chapter six.

Validity data found in a test manual can be of great value to the person attempting to select an appropriate aptitude test. However, once a test has been put into use, its validity for the specific purpose for which it is being employed should be studied regularly through the analysis of local data. For example, if it is being used to predict success in or group students for first-grade reading, a study should be made of the relationship between the intelligence test scores and the measure of reading achievement used in the local situation. The validity of an aptitude test depends not only on the characteristics of the test itself but also on the achievement measure used and on many aspects of the instructional situation.

Specific Uses for Intelligence Tests. Measures of scholastic aptitude or intelligence can be useful to teachers in a variety of ways and at a number of stages in a pupil's career. In general such measures can be helpful whenever it is important to know something about a pupil's potential for success in academic work.

Most schools administer some type of intelligence test at the end of kindergarten or before first grade. The results are helpful in making judgments as to how well the pupil can be expected to do first-grade work. In extreme cases they may suggest that the child should be placed in a special education class or remain in kindergarten for another year. For those students who are admitted to first grade they provide the teacher with some indication of what level of performance to expect. Where some type of grouping is employed and where pupils start instruction in reading at varying times, depending upon their ability, intelligence test scores are important aids in making various decisions.

It should again be emphasized that these scores should not be used in any arbitrary or rigid manner. Decisions should not be made solely on the basis of an MA or an IQ, and absolute cut-off scores should not be employed. These measures provide extremely useful information, but it is only one type of information and academic achievement depends on a great number of factors.

As a pupil progresses through school, teachers at all grade levels will find it helpful to know something about his academic aptitude. Considerable information will be provided by the student's record of achievement, by his grades, and by his scores on achievement tests. However, in some cases a record of past achievement is not a true indicator of a student's aptitude, and the teacher who wishes to know whether he is really helping the student to work to capacity will find intelligence test results a useful source of supplementary information.

In the junior high and high school years scores from intelligence tests are useful to the teacher and guidance counselor in assisting the student to make career decisions. By this time the student who has been enrolled in typical school systems will have taken intelligence tests at three or four points during his school career, and his general aptitude will have been established with some degree of reliability. This record of aptitude test results together with his record of achievement can provide some indication of his chances for success in specialized types of courses in the high school, in various types of post–high school study, and in different occupations and professions. This information should be weighed together with his interests and other factors in making career plans and decisions.

OTHER APTITUDE TESTS

Although tests of general mental ability or intelligence are much more widely used than is any other type of aptitude test, certain other tests are in considerable use. These include readiness tests, tests of aptitude for specific subjects, and aptitude-test batteries.

Readiness Tests. First-grade teachers frequently find tests of *reading readiness* or of *general readiness* for school instruction useful supplements to tests of intelligence in providing information about pupil aptitude. Although intelligence tests are useful in predicting reading achievement, instruments that are specifically constructed as reading-readiness tests can be more directly centered on abilities needed for learning to read. For example, the Metropolitan Readiness Tests [3] have six subtests that contribute to a total score that can be used for determining readiness for first-grade instruction. These subtests are: (1) word meaning—a measure of

---

3. Gertrude H. Hildreth, Nellie L. Griffiths, and Mary E. McGauvran, *Metropolitan Readiness Tests* (New York: Harcourt, Brace & World, 1949).

vocabulary which involves having the child mark the picture identified by a spoken word; (2) listening—a measure of listening comprehension requiring the examinee to mark the picture that depicts the action or situation described orally; (3) matching—a measure of ability to see similarities in pictured objects or groups of letters or numbers; (4) alphabet—a measure of ability to identify printed letters; (5) numbers—a measure of various types of knowledge of numbers; and (6) copying—a measure of visual perception and motor control.

Although test publishers point out that the total score from all tests combined is more reliable than subtest scores and should be given the most emphasis, they do suggest that some useful clues as to specific difficulties of poorer students may be obtained by looking at subtest scores.

Most readiness tests are somewhat similar to the Metropolitan, although some confine themselves to measuring readiness for reading only. Although scores from such tests generally do not correlate more highly with later achievement than do scores from intelligence tests, they have the advantage of providing some general diagnostic information that may be suggestive of remedial steps that the teacher might employ.

Tests of Aptitude for Specific Subjects. When students enter high school, decisions must be made as to whether they should enroll in certain courses or in certain sequenced programs of study. Such questions as the following will be raised: Can this student be expected to master a foreign language? Does this student have the aptitude needed in typing and shorthand? Should this student enroll in algebra or should he be encouraged to take a general mathematics course? The student's record in related courses that he has already taken will be useful, but a test of aptitude for the specific subject may also be of considerable help. A number of such tests have been developed to meet this need. The manuals for these tests present validity data indicating how scores correlate with a variety of measures of achievement. The school or the individual teacher using any of these instruments should make a study of how valid it is in the local situation. In some cases they have been found to be quite valid as predictors of success. In many situations, however, they have been found to be no more useful than the already available measures of general scholastic aptitude.

Aptitude Test Batteries. A test of aptitude for a certain subject can be useful when a student is concerned about how well he would do in that specific subject. Often, however, the concern of the student, or of the teacher or parent, is much broader than this and concerns the student's relative aptitude for a number of possible courses of study. Information of this nature can be helpful when the student is planning his school program and investigating possible vocations. This information might be secured by administering a number of separate aptitude tests for each of many specific subjects. However, such a procedure would not be very economical and probably would not provide a very meaningful basis for determining relative aptitude since each test would have been standardized on a different norm sample.

To meet this broader need, aptitude test batteries have been developed, composed of a certain number of subtests each of which measures aptitude for more than one course or vocation and all of which have been standardized on the same normative group. They are somewhat comparable to achievement test batteries in that they provide a rather complete set of tests that can be administered in a feasible amount of school time and provide a means whereby a student's score on one subtest can be compared meaningfully with his score on another.

Perhaps the best known example of an aptitude test battery is the Differential Aptitude Tests (DAT).[4] This instrument is made up of eight subtests: (1) verbal reasoning, (2) numerical ability, (3) abstract reasoning, (4) clerical speed and accuracy, (5) mechanical reasoning, (6) space relations, (7) language usage (spelling), and (8) language usage (sentences). The total battery can be administered in six class periods and the manual suggests that these can be distributed over two, three, or six days. Scores from the DAT are typically recorded on the individual report form as a profile, shown in Figure 26, which permits an easy determination of relative strengths and weaknesses in a pupil's aptitudes. The manual for DAT presents rather extensive data concerning the validity of the various subtests for predicting achievement in different school subjects. From these data the test user can determine what scores to employ in estimating a pupil's potential for success in any given

---

4. G. K. Bennett, H. G. Seashore, and A. G. Wesman, *Differential Aptitude Tests* (New York: The Psychological Corporation, 1962).

FIGURE 26

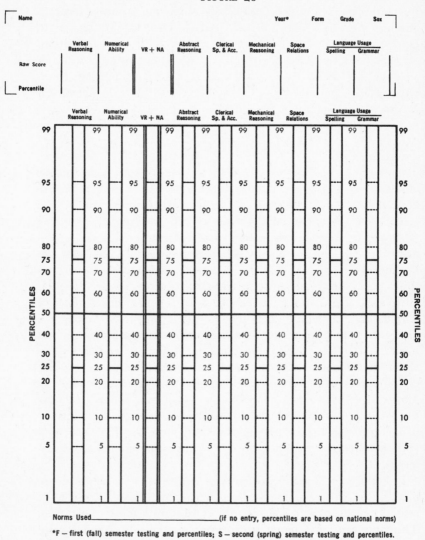

Profile Chart for Recording DAT Test Results. *Differential Aptitude Tests.* Reproduced by permission. Copyright © 1961, 1963, The Psychological Corporation, New York. All rights reserved.

subject. He will find, however, that the size of the predictive validity coefficient will vary considerably from one school system to another. This again suggests the need for local validity studies to determine the affectiveness of a test for the local school situation.

In addition to DAT there are several other aptitude batteries available for use in educational and vocational counseling. Interested persons will find these described and evaluated in the Mental Measurements yearbooks.

SUMMARY

There are many situations in which the teacher or other educator will find it important to have information concerning a pupil's aptitude for some type of schoolwork. Much information will be gained from an examination of the pupil's past record in school. However, for a variety of reasons, it is frequently useful to supplement information provided by past performance with data that can be gained from an aptitude test. The most widely used measure of this type is the test of general scholastic aptitude or intelligence. Such tests, which can be traced back to the pioneering work of Alfred Binet, include both individual and group tests. Among the group tests are instruments that yield only one measure (a general *mental age* or *intelligence quotient*), other tests that yield both a verbal and a nonverbal score, and still others that provide scores on a number of factors of intelligence. What instrument will be most valuable for a given purpose can be investigated by studying the validity data published with such tests, but the final answer to this question can be obtained only after the test has been used and the predictive validity for the local situation has been determined.

In addition to intelligence tests, certain other aptitude tests are used quite widely in the schools. These include readiness tests, tests of aptitude for a specific subject, and aptitude test batteries. The same cautions offered with respect to the use of intelligence tests are also applicable to the use of these instruments. It is important to remember that all these tests measure only a limited aspect of a student's potential and that many other sources of information must be given equal consideration.

Suggestions for Class Discussion and Further Investigation

1. Study the manuals for several intelligence tests, giving particular attention to the data on validity. What do these data suggest concerning the purposes for which a given test might be used? What other types of validity data might be helpful to you if you were considering using one of the tests?

2. Secure actual intelligence test scores (IQ's) and scores on some achievement test for a given group of pupils. Using procedures such as those used to develop the graphs in Figure 22 of chapter six, plot the relationship between IQ and achievement. Would IQ, as measured by this test, have been useful in grouping students in line with expected achievement in this subject? What conditions and factors may have kept this relationship from being larger than it is?

3. Make a careful study of the content of the test items of a given intelligence test. Where would an examinee have acquired the abilities required by these items? What types of background and experience might handicap an examinee in making a good score on this test?

4. The table below presents correlation data for some hypothetical tests. Assume that both readiness tests were administered during the early part of first grade and that the achievement test was given near the end of first grade. Each correlation coefficient represents the correlation between the test named in that column and the test named in that row.

	Pit Readiness Tests, Form A			Blank Achievement Tests	
	Reading	Numbers	Total	Reading	Arithmetic
Pit Readiness Tests, Form B					
Reading	0.89	0.42	0.62	0.44	0.41
Numbers	0.39	0.92	0.57	0.34	0.57
Total	0.60	0.55	0.88	0.65	0.61

Using the technical terminology of validity and reliability where appropriate, explain what each correlation coefficient in this table would tell you about these tests.

Suggestions for Further Reading

The following sources give interesting and useful information on the history of intelligence testing: Rudolph Pintner, *Intelligence Testing* (New York: Holt, Rinehart and Winston, 1923); George D. Stoddard, *The Meaning of Intelligence* (New York: Macmillan, 1943); Lewis M. Terman, *The Measurement of Intelligence* (Boston: Houghton Mifflin Co., 1916).

Rather complete discussions of various types of intelligence test and other aptitude tests are found in the widely used texts: Anne Anastasi, *Psychological Testing* (New York: Macmillan, 1954) and Lee J. Cronbach, *Essentials of Psychological Testing*, 2nd ed. (New York: Harper & Row, 1960).

Essential materials for study with this chapter are tests and test manuals for a number of group intelligence tests. These can be secured from a school's test library or by requesting copies from the publisher. In reviewing such materials the reader should also have available Oscar K. Buros, ed., *The Sixth Mental Measurements Yearbook* (Highland Park, N.J.: Gryphon Press, 1965).

Chapter Nine

Using an Evaluation Program

If tests and other evaluation procedures are to be used effectively, their use must be planned as an integral part of weekly and daily lesson plans. After studying certain materials or having some other specified learning experience, a student's achievement of the related objectives should be assessed by some specific evaluation procedure. He should be expected to take a test, work certain problems, answer given questions, or demonstrate his proficiency through some type of performance. In some cases such evaluations will cover things that have been learned in as brief a period as one day, while in other cases they may cover an entire unit or a school term. Planning must also include the specification of the time and the purposes for the administration of any standardized achievement or aptitude tests to be used. Detailed planning of this type is essential if tests are not to become rather meaningless ends in themselves rather than integral elements in the instructional program. This chapter will discuss the basic features of an integrated program of testing and evaluation, present brief descriptions of some useful nontesting procedures, and describe certain ways of using the information obtained.

USING ACHIEVEMENT TESTS

The typical teacher can make profitable use of a variety of types of achievement test. These will include relatively short quizzes, longer tests covering a complete unit of study or an entire semester, and standardized tests that may be made up of a variety of different subtests. If all these tests are to serve the important purposes that they can serve, their use must be planned to provide the desired information at the time when it is needed.

At the start of a school term the teacher needs information about what each pupil has mastered and what he is ready to study next. The frequent assumption that all students in a given class are ready to start at the same point is quite unjustified in view of our knowledge of individual differences among students. The use of tests to *place* pupils at the proper point in the curriculum sequence is important in any type of classroom, and if the present trend toward the individualization of instruction continues it will be of growing importance in the classrooms of the future. Standardized achievement tests given at the start of the year may be of some use for this placement. However, if the educational program is to do an effective job in taking past learning into account in planning the work of individual pupils, it is likely that special placement tests may have to be developed for a given curriculum. In any event, every teacher's program of testing and evaluation should include some provision for using test results to determine where instruction should begin for each pupil.

If, as is typical, course content is organized in units of study, it should be helpful to give each student a *pretest* as he starts a given unit. That is, even after it has been decided, on the basis of some type of placement data, that a student should begin his study with a given unit, it is useful to obtain additional information concerning his capabilities with respect to any of the specific content of that unit. This information can be used in prescribing what materials he should work with and in deciding what materials he may be able to skip in studying that unit. A wider use of pretesting could make instruction much more efficient.

One of the most common and most important uses of tests is in the frequent and regular *assessment of each pupil's progress* as he works through a unit. This may include the use of a number of short tests or quizzes, each one covering material that the student may master in one or a few class periods. Such tests should include items dealing with each of the behavioral objectives toward which the study materials are directed. Tests of this type are sometimes referred to as "curriculum embedded tests" because they are an integral and an essential part of the curriculum sequence and because they should be viewed by the student as another element in the set of lesson materials. Planning for and developing quizzes of this type represents a major part of the evaluation task of the teacher. They should be developed at the same time that study materials are being developed. Assume, for example, that an instructional objective states that "the pupil should be able to punctuate a compound sentence correctly." In planning for this part of a unit of work the teacher must develop or locate study and practice exercises that the student will use in mastering this objective, and, as a closely related step, should also identify test exercises that can be used to assess the achievement of this ability. This development of study and test materials as a part of the same process is an important procedure in achieving an integrated and meaningful program of evaluation. In some cases the teacher's task is simplified by using published study materials such as workbook exercises that include frequent quizzes as a part of the sequence. Uses for the results of quizzes are quite obvious. They provide information for both the student and the teacher as to how well the student is doing in each step of the work. Such information is useful in day-by-day planning and in the diagnoses of the strengths and weaknesses of the individual student as well as of the instructional materials.

Periodically the teacher will wish to employ tests that cover relatively large segments of the course, such as *unit tests* or *end-of-course examinations.* These are an essential supplement to the shorter quizzes, for they can be used to determine whether the pupil has combined ideas from several lessons into broader learnings and to assess his retention over some period of time. Results from such tests are used to make decisions as to whether a pupil has mastered a given unit and is ready to move on to something new. Where the unit being assessed is essentially an entire school year, it may be possible to secure a standardized test that will be useful for this purpose.

OTHER EVALUATION PROCEDURES

The teacher will use a variety of nontesting evaluation procedures for some of the purposes served by achievement testing. He will check pupil worksheets, examine assigned exercises and problems, grade homework, quiz pupils orally, and observe pupils as they perform. Although these procedures are typically carried out in a somewhat less formal manner than is achievement testing, if their use is planned carefully they can be essential elements in the teacher's evaluation program. These nontesting methods will be the only procedures that will give the teacher valid information regarding pupil achievement of certain types of objectives. However, a major weakness of most such procedures is their lack of reliability and objectivity when they are employed in the rather casual fashion of many teachers. These deficiencies can be reduced, however, if the teacher is conscious of them and makes use of certain strategies and techniques.

Some simple nontesting procedures such as the grading of classwork and homework assignments can be made to produce more reliable information if some of the same steps are used here as are used with essay examinations. This means that great care must be employed in phrasing the assignment and in planning the scoring method. The aim should be to produce a more objective assessment of the pupils' work.

A more difficult job of evaluation is involved in cases where the desired pupil behavior does not produce a tangible product but is some performance that can be observed or listened to only at the time that the pupil is exhibiting it. Objectives of this type include the ability to give a speech, participate in a discussion, perform some type of athletic feat, sing, or play a musical instrument. When a pupil exhibits these abilities, his performance does not result in a paper that can be scored or in some other tangible product that can be assessed and re-examined several times if necessary. His performance must be evaluated through the use of a subjective and rather instantaneous judgment of its value, making a reliable evaluation more difficult. To improve the objectivity and the reliability of the assessment of pupil achievement in many situations where observational methods must be used, certain techniques described in the following sections may be helpful to the teacher.

Rating Scales. One of the most useful nontesting evaluation devices is the rating scale. This can be particularly helpful where the behavior being evaluated is made up of several different aspects each of which can be a dimension on the rating instrument. For example, in assessing the ability of a student to present a speech to the class, the teacher would be concerned with several separate aspects of the total performance. Some of these are suggested by the simple rating scale shown on page 170.

In using this device the teacher would give careful attention to a pupil as he is speaking and then decide which descriptive category comes closest to describing his performance for each dimension. A check mark would then be placed on the scale above the pertinent description. This place on the scale or the numerical

RATING SCALE FOR CLASSROOM SPEECH

Pupil's name _____ Date _____

Speech topic _____

1. Did the speech contain content meaningful to the topic?

1	2	3	4
Most of speech content not truly meaningful	Only about 50 percent of speech relevant	Most content relevant; occasional irrelevant idea	All content obviously and clearly related

2. Was the delivery smooth and unhesitating?

1	2	3	4
Long pauses and groping for words in almost every sentence	Pauses and groping for words in about 50 percent of sentences	Occasional pause and groping for words	Delivery smooth; no pauses or groping for words

3. Did the speaker use correct grammar?

1	2	3	4
Errors in most sentences	Errors in about 50 percent of sentences	From 1 to 3 errors	No errors

4. Did the speaker look at his audience?

1	2	3	4
Looked away most of the time	Looked at audience only 50 percent of the time	Looked at audience most of the time	Looked continually at audience

value associated with it would then represent the pupil's rating on the dimension.

This total scale deals with four separate aspects of a speaking performance and provides for rating the student on each of the four dimensions. This division serves to call the teacher's attention to these aspects, and the total scale, when marked, provides a rather descriptive but simple record of the pupil's performance. It can serve as a basis for specific suggestions to the pupil, and, if it is filled out each time a pupil presents a speech, the series of ratings can be used to note changes in a pupil's performance.

As suggested before, a rating instrument of this type can be used in assessing many types of achievement. In some cases, the teacher may find useful published devices. More frequently, however, it will be necessary to develop the desired scale. This may be done by one teacher or may be a cooperative venture of several teachers with a common need. In making an instrument of this type it is first necessary to decide what aspects of the total performance are to constitute dimensions. What are the important things to observe or to listen for? Each such dimension may be defined by some specific question such as those used in the scale presented here. The points along each dimension are then identified by brief descriptions. One should start by describing the two extreme categories, the very best and the very poorest performances. Following this one describes the intermediate points. The number of descriptive categories or points on the scale that should be used will depend to some extent on how many distinctly different performances it is possible to identify. Usually four or five such categories will be used.

In writing the descriptive categories it is important to be clear and specific. Each one should be so unambiguous that different raters observing the same performance could be expected to agree on the rating to be assigned. That is, subjectivity is to be reduced to a minimum. Scales are sometimes developed in such a way that each point on the scale is described by only one word such as "always," "frequently," "never," and "seldom." Such scales are of little value since words such as "frequently" and "seldom" do not have a specific meaning and the rating to be assigned depends too much on the subjective judgment of the rater.

Rating scales represent one of the most useful evaluation devices available to the teacher and probably should be used much more widely. Their use can introduce a degree of specificity and objectivity into the assessment of many types of achievement that are too often evaluated through highly unreliable procedures. The major advantages of rating scales may be summarized as follows:

1. They provide a uniform set of the essential aspects of a performance constituting the specific qualities to be observed.

2. The use of specific descriptive categories to identify the various points along a dimension greatly improves the objectivity and reliability of scores assigned.

3. The dimensions and descriptive categories provide a useful basis for offering suggestions for improvement.

4. The filled-in scale provides a permanent record of a given performance. Such a record can be very useful in studying pupil progress. It also provides a basis for a re-examination and re-appraisal of a given performance if this is needed in discussions with pupils or parents or in such decisions as determining an over-all grade.

Check Lists. Another simple evaluative device that can be used as an aid to observation is the check list. This is useful where some type of desired pupil performance is made up of several steps or parts but each part can only be judged as either present or absent rather than given a rating. Shown below is a brief check list that might be used in observing whether a sewing student has learned all the steps necessary to set up a machine so that it is ready for sewing.

CHECK LIST FOR FIRST STEPS
IN PREPARING TO SEW ON A MACHINE

Name of student _____ *Date* _____

_____1. Wind bobbin	_____6. Insert fabric under
_____2. Thread bobbin case	presser foot
_____3. Thread upper machine	_____7. Position needle in fabric
_____4. Pull up bobbin thread	_____8. Lower presser foot
_____5. Set stitch length	

This instrument might be useful to the teacher in assessing pupil performance and to the pupil in analyzing his own mastery of the required steps. It can be an important aid to instruction in that it calls attention to all the essential steps in a performance.

It can also be used for marking pupils merely by assigning a score representing the number of steps that the pupil has mastered and remembers to execute.

Check lists can be constructed for use in evaluating a variety of abilities. The above example suggests that these are easily applied to the assessment of a pupil's ability to operate equipment or machines. Physical-education teachers find them useful in analyzing a pupil's ability to carry out an athletic feat that is made up of several component parts. For example, a check list for assessing a beginning performance in tennis might include such items as "hits forehand stroke," "hits backhand," "serves," and similar basic parts of the game. Similarly, shop teachers use such a device in connection with operations that may be considered as consisting of several component parts.

Check lists may also be useful for assessing pupil "products," that is, for checking to see whether something the pupil produces contains all the essential elements. For example, a woodshop teacher might make his evaluation of a piece of furniture built by a student more objective and reliable by employing a check list containing such items as the following:

_____Dimensions are accurate within allowed limits
_____Parts are fitted together as per drawings
_____Joints are tight
_____Surfaces show proper sanding
_____Finish is applied evenly and smoothly
_____Surfaces are rubbed to proper finish

Comparable check lists could be developed for evaluating written products such as business letters, outlines, and plans for an experiment.

Anecdotal Records.   Certain types of instructional objectives that must be evaluated by observation of behavior cannot be divided into dimensions and rated on scales or check lists. The behavior can only be described and given a general assessment. In the evaluation of such objectives *anecdotal records* may be of some use. An anecdotal record is a brief written description of some specific behavior or action that was observed by the writer. If the behavior observed and recorded represents evidence of the extent to which the pupil has mastered some objective, a series of such records can provide valuable data on pupil progress. For example, let us assume that one objective that an elementary school teacher might have for her science teaching was that "the pupil will develop enough interest in science so that during his free periods he will choose to read science books or to work with some of the science equipment." She might do certain things to stimulate this interest and then observe what a pupil does during a free period. Brief anecdotal records could then be used to note any progress shown by an individual student. A series of anecdotes for one student might be something like the following.

November 3, 10:30 A.M.
End of arithmetic lesson
When Paul completed his arithmetic, I told him he could do anything he wished for the next ten minutes. He went to the reading table and looked at the covers of three or four different books. Then he returned to his seat and gazed out the window until reading period started.

November 7, 10:30 A.M.
End of arithmetic lesson
Paul completed his assignment and I told him that he could do what he wished. He went to the reading table and leafed through two books. He then went to the science shelf and played with a magnet for about two minutes. After this he returned to his seat and rested with his head on his desk.

November 9, 10:25 A.M.
Since Paul had finished his arithmetic test, I told him that he would have fifteen minutes of free time. He returned to his desk and gazed out the window for two or three minutes. Then he went to the science shelf and spent about five minutes seeing how many nails he could pick up with the horseshoe magnet.

In this illustration the three anecdotes seem to show that Paul is developing some interest in using his free time to work with the science equipment. The teacher might note this progress through casual and unrecorded observation but the use of written anecdotes forces one to note and record specific evidence. The anecdotes also provide a written record that can be examined from time to time to reassess progress and can be shown to another teacher, a supervisor, parents, or the pupil himself. It permits any interested person to "see" what the pupil has been doing.

Anecdotal records will probably not be used too widely by the classroom teacher since writing them can be time consuming and since there are only a few types of objectives for which they are appropriate. Such records will probably be used only with selected students. In the situation described above, for example, anecdotes would not have to be written for those pupils who always displayed a great interest in working with science equipment. It could merely be noted that they had achieved the objective, and the recording effort could then be concentrated on those pupils in whom the interest had yet to be generated. Also, the teacher might find it necessary to do some time sampling by observing two or three pupils on one day, another two or three on a second day, and so on, so that the pupils first observed might not be observed a second time until four or five days later. Although this would not provide a complete record of what any pupil did, it should be sufficient to detect any trends in his behavior patterns.

It is generally suggested that each written anecdote should be placed on a separate small card and that such cards should be placed in the individual pupil's folder. The behavior described should be behavior that is relevant to the objective that is being evaluated. Statements should be limited to specific, factual descriptions of what took place. The anecdote should not evaluate the behavior as good or bad. Neither should the anecdote contain statements that attempt to explain the reasons for a behavior. These are separate steps to be carried out after the anecdotes have been read and studied. An anecdote is merely a "picture" of a pertinent instance of some behavior and might be considered as an economical substitute for a sound motion picture of what took place.

SUMMARIZING EVALUATION RESULTS

For certain purposes it is necessary that teachers combine the results from several different tests or other evaluation procedures to secure some total or summarizing figure for each pupil. For example, let us assume that during instruction on one particular unit of study a teacher checked pupil progress at various points by using two different quizzes, scores on an assigned homework paper, and ratings on a special rating scale. How can the teacher combine a pupil's scores from these four assessments into one measure that will indicate how well he did on the total unit? The teacher is also faced with the need for this type of summarizing measure when he combines scores from a variety of assessments in order to determine a pupil's course grade. What is the fairest way of arriving at this figure?

A Suggested Procedure for Summarizing Data. The problem in summarizing evaluation results can perhaps best be seen by reference to some illustrative data. The following results, based on four measures used in the hypothetical unit mentioned previously, are an example of what might appear in a teacher's grade book or a similar record source.

	Quiz 1	Paper		Rating	Quiz 2
Art A.	50	A–	(9)	5	25
Billy B.	46	B+	(8)	5	26
Chris C.	41	A	(10)	4	29
Donna D.	44	A–	(9)	5	27
Eve E.	38	B	(7)	2	22
Frank F.	33	C	(4)	3	20
George G.	26	C+	(5)	3	21
Harry H.	30	B	(7)	3	17
Ida I.	22	D	(1)	4	16
John J.	20	C	(4)	3	14

How can these four measures be combined to provide an overall measure of pupil performance on this unit, or how can these and additional measures eventually be combined to yield a score or grade for the work of a total semester? If we merely attempted to add the four results for any one student we would have certain difficulties. First of all, we cannot add letters and numbers; consequently, a first step would be to translate the letter grades assigned to the paper to some type of numerical measure. We might think of assigning 5 to an "A," 4 to a "B," and so on, but this would leave us with the problem of assigning fractional values to such marks as "A –" and "B +." A more simple procedure is to assign the numeral 1 to the lowest grade used ("D," in this case) and number consecutively on up through the higher grades. This would mean that in this case a "D +" has a value of 2, "C –" a value of 3, "C" a value of 4, and so on. The resulting numerical values have been inserted in parentheses to the right of each letter grade in our table of data.

At first thought it might seem that once all marks are in numerical form a meaningful summary can be obtained merely by finding a total for each student. However, this step could give an inaccurate picture and be quite unfair to some students because of the differences in the size of scores and in the variability or range of scores on the four different procedures used. In our example, scores on quiz 1 would have a much greater weight and influence on a student's total than any of the other three measures merely because the scores are larger and extend over a wider range. Similarly, a pupil's score on the "rating" would have little weight or influence on the total. Now it is likely that the teacher would feel that these different measures should carry different weights, but this differentiation should be determined on the basis of the relative importance of what is covered by the evaluation procedure rather than solely by the range of scores that it happens to produce. Hence, a first step in combining scores is to equate the weights of the various measures involved. Following this, if the measures are to be assigned differential importance, the scores on some of the measures can be multiplied by logically determined weights.

A variety of procedures are available to equate scores from different evaluation devices. All involve a conversion to some type of derived score. These (discussed in chapter five) include such scores as the percentile rank, the z-score, and the stanine score. Any one of these would serve to make our four measures relatively equivalent. For purposes of illustration we shall use the percentile rank. Shown below is the same portion of a teacher's grade book that was presented before but with all the scores converted to percentile ranks. (The student should review the computational procedure described in chapter five and check the figures presented here by recomputing each set of percentile ranks.)

	Quiz 1	Paper (wt. 2)	Rating	Quiz 2 (wt. 2)	Weighted total
Art A.	95	80	85	65	470
Billy B.	85	65	85	75	450
Chris C.	65	95	60	95	505
Donna D.	75	80	85	85	490
Eve E.	55	50	5	55	270
Frank F.	45	20	30	35	185
George G.	25	35	30	45	215
Harry H.	35	50	30	25	215
Ida I.	15	5	60	15	115
John J.	5	20	30	5	85

If the teacher chooses to arrive at a total for each student by adding his four scores, each of the four measures would be given approximately equal weight. Let us assume, however, that the "paper" and "quiz 2" are judged to be of greater importance in assessing the pupils' ability than are the other two measures. The decision may then be made to give them twice the weight of the others. This could be done by doubling each pupil's score on the "paper" and on "quiz 2" before adding the four scores together. In our illustration this has been done and the "weighted total" has been entered in the righthand column. The relative size of these totals then tells us each student's position within this class group as far as his overall mastery of the content of this unit is concerned.

Preparing Reports and Grades.   An accepted teacher's task is that of preparing reports and records that provide information concerning pupil progress and achievement. The most typical form of such reports is the traditional report card, which is intended to convey information about pupil achievement to the parent, the pupil himself, other teachers, and, perhaps, prospective employers.

Although the traditional report card, containing a letter grade for each subject the pupil is taking, is undoubtedly the most widely used form for conveying this information, a great number of other procedures have been developed and are being used. Some schools report to parents through private conferences of the parent, the teacher, and perhaps the pupil. Others provide time to allow the teacher to write a personal letter to each pupil's parents describing his progress and his difficulties. Many schools have devoted considerable time to the development of a report card that seems to fit their particular needs. Some of the more complete forms provide for reporting letter grades and scores on standardized achievement tests as well as verbal descriptions of some of the pupil's characteristics. Persons or groups designing a special report card form for their local situation should make an effort to examine as many forms as possible so that they will not overlook any unique features that may be of real value in a given situation.

Assigning Letter Grades.   Despite the imaginative variety of new reporting procedures that have been proposed and given some trial, the traditional letter grade is still an essential element in the report cards used by most schools. That is, most schools employ a traditional-type card that uses only the letter grade, or they employ a modified system that provides some variety of types of information, including letter grades as one of the types. For this reason it is important that every teacher have some command of a valid procedure for assigning letter grades.

In using letter grades it is important to remember that since their only purpose is to convey information their meaning must be clear to everyone concerned. It should be possible for a teacher, if he is called upon to do so, to explain rather exactly what a grade of "A," "B," or "E" means. It also suggests that any report card that uses such grades should contain an explanation of what they mean or how they are derived. Some teachers tend to use letter grades as though each had some absolute meaning and as though the teacher is to determine through intuition the letter grade to assign to a given pupil or performance. They make judgments such as "That is a 'B' paper" or "He is a 'C' pupil" without having a rationale for defending the judgment or without being able to explain the real meaning of the grade.

The most widely used, meaningful procedure for assigning grades is the definition of each grade in terms of percentage of students who typically receive it. This is sometimes referred to as "grading on the curve" since it can be thought of as a derivation from the normal curve procedure for grading.[1] There is rather widespread agreement among persons who have given considerable thought to the problem of assigning grades that all procedures that have any real meaning ultimately define each letter in terms of percentage of pupils who receive it and who are above and below it. The meaning of such grades can be defined and hence they can fulfill their purpose of conveying information. Of course, there must be some common agreement within a school or school system as to the percentage of pupils that should be assigned each grade. There is no standard or "scientific" procedure for determining such percentages and they may differ among school levels. That is, the percentage distribution in graduate school will probably be quite different from what it is in college or in high school. The actual percentages used in any particular school or system can be decided

---

1. The author has discussed this procedure in some detail in *Testing and Evaluation: An Introduction* (New York: Harcourt, Brace & World, 1961), pp. 253–56.

quite arbitrarily but will probably be based somewhat on tradition and on common usage.

To see what assumptions are made in following this procedure and exactly how the procedure can be applied, consider this example. Let us assume that a school has defined the letter grades as follows:

> "A" top 15 percent
> "B" next 25 percent
> "C" next 35 percent
> "D" next 15 percent
> "E" bottom 10 percent

It should be understood that percentages such as these provide a general definition of the grades but do not have to be applied exactly every year or to every class. This distribution is a guide suggesting what percentage of pupils will receive each grade if we consider all pupils in the school taken over a period of years. Individual teachers may have to make minor adjustments from class to class and from year to year depending on the aptitude of the specific group being graded. That is, if a teacher has a class he feels is rather typical of the school as far as academic aptitude and general ability is concerned, he would probably stay quite close to the established percentages in assigning grades. If he had a second class of students who were generally superior in overall ability, he would want to increase the "A" and "B" percentages and reduce the percentages given the lower grades. Similarly, the reverse of this type of adjustment would be made with a class that was below average in general performance.

In applying this procedure for assigning grades the teacher must first have a valid basis for arranging the students in an order corresponding with their relative performance in the class. This order will, of course, be based on an accumulation of all the evidence gathered during the particular school term. Such evidence may include test scores, scores on homework assignments, ratings on class performance, and results from the use of other evaluative procedures. How all these measures can be combined into a "weighted total" was explained and illustrated in the preceding section of this chapter. After such a weighted total has been calculated for each pupil, all students are ranked in order according to these totals.

Let us assume that carrying out this procedure for a class of 36 students results in the order shown below. Taking the agreed-upon

Pupil	Weighted total		Pupil	Weighted total	
1	426		19	328	
2	415		20	322	
3	409	"A"	21	320	
4	397		22	317	
5	392		23	313	"C"
6	390		24	307	
7	375		25	306	
8	371		26	298	
9	368		27	294	
10	368		28	280	
11	362	"B"	29	278	"D"
12	357		30	271	
13	349		31	267	
14	345		32	248	
15	341		33	245	
16	336		34	244	"E"
17	334	"C"	35	236	
18	330		36	219	

percentages of 36 we find that 5.4 pupils should get "A," 9 should get "B," 12.6 "C," 5.4 "D," and 3.6 "E." If this class happens to be rather typical of the school as far as general performance is concerned, we can use these figures as starting points in assigning grades. Knowing that we should have 5 or 6 "A"s, we count down from the top and note that, as far as weighted total is concerned, there is a much bigger difference between the sixth and seventh pupils than between the fifth and sixth. This would probably result in our giving "A" to the top 6. It is relatively simple to decide that the next 9 should receive "B" and the following 12 should get "C." If we use the suggested percentage of "D," 5 or possibly 6 persons will receive that grade. However, since the weighted totals for pupils 32, 33, and 34 are all quite close, it would seem more reasonable to have the dividing line between "D" and "E" fall between students 31 and 32. This seems to be a justifiable procedure although the resulting 4 "D"s and 5 "E"s represent a slight departure from the suggested numbers for these two grades.

The presentation of this procedure for assigning letter grades does not mean it is always the most desirable method. It is *one* method that gives some easily explainable meaning to letter grades. In situations where other procedures seem more desirable, the teacher should make certain that parents and students can be given some equally simple explanation of the meaning of assigned grades.

SUMMARY

Evaluation devices can be used with maximum effectiveness only if their use is planned on a long-range basis as a part of the development of the total instructional program. This plan should indicate the times or the points in the sequence at which achievement is to be assessed, the exact procedures to be employed, and the purposes for which results are to be used. If the instructional program is designed to meet the needs of the individual student, it will be found that achievement measures will be essential for such things as (1) placing the pupil at the proper point in the learning sequence, (2) planning a program fitted to his capabilities, (3) keeping a careful check on his progress, and (4) determining when he has mastered given units of instruction. The teacher who is going to use evaluation devices for all the important purposes they can serve should be capable not only of constructing a variety of types of tests but also of developing and applying such useful nontesting techniques as rating scales, check lists, and anecdotal records. Results from many such procedures together with assessments of such standard items as homework assignments, class exercises, term reports, and so forth, will have to be used if the teacher is to obtain a comprehensive picture of pupil attainment. All the obtained results will then have to be combined in some meaningful manner for purposes of reporting overall progress to the student, his parents, and other teachers. This chapter has attempted to offer certain suggestions as to how an evaluation program can be used to achieve these ends.

Suggestions for Class Discussion and Further Investigation

1. Use the "rating scale for classroom speech" on page 170 to rate some speaking performance that you can observe. (If this is used as an exercise for a total class it can be carried out by having one or more students present short speeches in class.) What aspects of a speaking performance are not

covered by these dimensions? Develop additional scales to rate these aspects.

2. Develop a "check list" of the type shown on page 173 that could be used for rating the quality of a teacher-made objective test. Items in the list might include such things as "adequate instructions," "specific provisions for marking answers," etc. Use the check list to assess a test you developed for this course. What important qualities of a test cannot be assessed by a check list?

3. Pupils in graduate schools typically are given grades of "A," "B," or "C." What might be the justification for such a practice?

4. Secure copies of as many different types of report card as possible. How many different procedures for assigning grades are represented on these cards? Does each card provide a meaningful interpretation of the grades?

Suggestions for Further Reading

More complete discussions of the use of rating scales, check lists, anecdotal records, and other aids to observation as an evaluation procedure will be found in J. Stanley Ahmann and Marvin D. Glock, *Evaluating Pupil Growth* (Boston: Allyn & Bacon, 1958), ch. 14; Norman E. Gronlund, *Measurement and Evaluation in Teaching* (New York: Macmillan, 1965), ch. 16; R. M. Thomas, *Judging Student Progress* (New York: David McKay Co., 1960), chs. 8 and 11.

A variety of suggestions concerning marking and grading procedures will be found in C. M. Lindvall, *Testing and Evaluation: An Introduction* (New York: Harcourt, Brace & World, 1961), appendix; Alfred Schwartz and Stuart C. Tiedeman, *Evaluating Student Progress in the Secondary School* (New York: David McKay Co., 1957), ch. 18; Ann Z. Smith and J. E. Dobbins, "Marks and Marking Systems," *Encyclopedia of Educational Research,* 3rd ed. (New York: Macmillan, 1960), pp. 783–89; R. M. Thomas, *op. cit.,* chs. 13–15.

Index

185